Discipline and Moral Education

A Survey of Public Opinion and Understanding

JOHN WILSON

NFER - Nelson

Published by The NFER-Nelson Publishing Company Ltd.,
Darville House, 2 Oxford Road East,
Windsor, Berks. SL4 1DF.

First Published 1981
©John Wilson, 1981
ISBN 0-85633-233-X
Code 8121 021

Photoset in Plantin by The Yale Press Ltd.
Printed in Great Britain.

Distributed in the USA by Humanities Press Inc.,
Atlantic Highlands, New Jersey 07716 USA

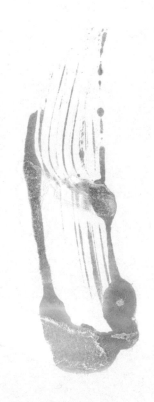

Discipline and Moral Education

Contents

Preface

This book has two purposes:
1. To present the origins, progress and conclusions of research in two connected areas or aspects of education, those marked by the terms 'discipline' and 'moral education' (ME: I shall use this abbreviation throughout).
2. To show, by means of this exemplar, how educational research ought – at least characteristically, and in the large majority of important cases – to be initially conducted.

It may be asked which of these purposes is the more important, but I do not see how that question can be easily answered. That there should be effective discipline and ME in schools is a matter of great and (for many societies) urgent practical significance: however, we cannot gain this and other objectives and retain them securely unless we go through certain procedures, or understand certain things; and these procedures and understandings are themselves enshrined in proper methods of research. This applies to almost any educational objectives, as we shall show later (Chapter 2).

So far as the first purpose is concerned, the basic, and perhaps ultimately the only, trouble is that the concepts marked by 'discipline' and 'ME' are not firmly grasped or properly understood by, or immediately available to, the minds of many people (particularly educationalists), though they can come to understand them under suitable guidance. Because of this, (a) certain other concepts connected with them (for instance, those marked by 'authority', 'obedience' and 'morality' as a form of thought) tend to disappear or at least become obfuscated, (b) educational research on these topics starts off on the wrong foot, and, not least important, (c) the actual *practice* of discipline and ME is inhibited or vitiated by this failure to understand their true nature. The first – and again, perhaps in a sense the only important – thing to be done, then, is that people in general, and educators in particular, should gain the required clarity. Much of our research is concerned with this process, and with showing what kinds of opinions and beliefs flow from a proper conceptual grasp.

So far as the second purpose is concerned, it has long been obvious that educational research is in an appalling muddle. This would not much matter if the muddle affected only the academic world; unfortunately it also affects teachers and other practical educators, not only by failing to help them in their work but also by infecting them with fashions of thought and supposed research findings, most of which no serious and intellectually competent person could regard as anything but dubious at best, and at worst as rubbish. The right kind of research requires far more seriousness, clarity and common sense than most researchers seem able, or willing, to display. I have defended this harsh judgement elsewhere (Wilson, J. 1972, 1979b); but I hope, perhaps with too much optimism, that a practical example will get the message across more effectively.

For reasons given in Chapter 1 it is best that both those concerned with conducting the research and those otherwise involved in it (apart from myself) remain anonymous; consequently I cannot thank them by name. But they will know how grateful I am. I must also express my thanks for their support to the trustees and associates of (a) the Farmington Trust, which was concerned with serious research into ME during the period 1965–72 (some of the thoughts and material, though much revised, in Chapters 5 and 6 date back to that period), and (b) of the Warborough Trust, formed after 1972 to continue such research.

Some other ideas and material in this book have appeared elsewhere in some form or other (I must in particular mention the remarks on the concept of discipline in Chapter 3 section 'A', which appear in my *Philosophy and Practical Education* – see reference); but the revision of this material and the need to work it into this particular project of research make me unapologetic about repeating myself. There is a permanent problem here for philosophers, who often want to make what is – in some skeletal sense – the same conceptual point in very different contexts: rather as mathematicians, for instance, use the same ('unoriginal') methods of addition, subtraction, etc. for solving very different problems. Everything depends on just *how* the point (the method) is deployed. I do not much mind if the reader regards some of what is said here as repetitious: my chief hope is that he will see how the methodological or philosophical points fit into, or make a framework for, empirical research as a matter of demonstrable practical importance and urgency.

J.B.W.
Oxford, 1981

Part One

CHAPTER ONE
Origins of the Research

In many ways this is the most important chapter of the book, because in educational research almost everything turns on *starting off* in the right way. But it is also the most difficult to write because 'starting off in the right way' involves many different kinds of consideration, the full force of which will only become apparent as the book proceeds. The reader must forgive me for setting out some of them rather brusquely.

A number of interesting experiences combined to thrust this research upon us. First, as Research Supervisor of the Warborough Trust (a body concerned generally with 'ME', in its broad sense), I had some desire and obligation to give teachers a firm grasp of some basic ideas and practices. Not only those marked by 'ME' but also those marked by 'discipline' seemed particularly important. Discipline might indeed be conceived as part of ME; and in any case how much, after all, could be achieved by sophisticated and delicate methods of ME in schools if these were not supported by firm and properly understood disciplinary structures? Secondly, as a lecturer and tutor in a university department of educational studies, I was responsible for the education of student-teachers and in-service teachers: not only did discipline and ME constantly crop up as topics for discussion, but it rapidly became obvious that none of us was really clear about them. Thirdly, the actual experience in schools of those of us who had been, or were, practising teachers showed (what is of course wholly obvious) that there were severely practical aspects to the problem. Finally, on consulting the literature, we failed to discover any books or 'research findings' which dealt at all adequately with 'discipline' (even philosphers who had written under that heading seemed to have got it wrong), and little serious empirical work which was really about moral education. All this suggested that it might be worthwhile if we attempted something ourselves.

By 'we' here, I refer to about twenty people who have been closely associated with this task over a period of some eight or nine years (roughly, since 1972). None of those concerned were directly connected with the Oxford Department of Educational Studies, so that neither that Department as a whole nor any individuals within it can be held responsible for what is here published. At the same time, I should record my gratitude for many useful informal conversations with colleagues and students within that particular Department. Most were practising teachers: of both sexes, various ages, and heterogeneous qualifications. We did not and could not, of course, regard this as anything like a full-time business, and it is virtually impossible to estimate the man-hours spent on it since much of the work was extremely informal. There were many other people more indirectly associated with it, as research subjects rather than as researchers: but this distinction is in fact hard to make either theoretically or in practice. For, as will shortly be apparent, much of the work necessarily consists in discovering *how a person sees* the world – what concepts he entertains, what words he marks them by and what values he attaches to them: and in this business the person is as much a co-researcher as a 'subject'.

When I add to this the facts that this research was not funded from any source, nor publicized in any way before or during its progress, the reader will easily perceive just how unlike it was to most research projects; and it is at this point, I think, that we may best take a direct look at certain basic *practical* conditions which are crucial to most educational research. The relevant points may be briefly summarized as follows:

1. There must be somebody with a sufficiently high level of 'philosophical' (to use a grand word) competence who, if he does not actually direct the work, at least makes sure that its general structure and methodology are sound. This at once became clear in the case of discipline: what books and research findings, supposedly about discipline, said was sometimes interesting and important but, since their authors lacked either the ability or the will to give an accurate account of the *subject* of their research (that is, of what ground the term 'discipline' actually covers) it was not clear how much they said which was interesting or important *for that subject*. They also used, unsurprisingly, quite inappropriate methodologies and techniques (see Chapter 2).

2. The members of the research team should know, trust and respect each other preferably *before* being identified or institu-

tionalized as a team. Much of the work consists, necessarily, of informal discussion and interaction, in which there has to be a good deal of fairly sophisticated cut-and-thrust argument and trenchant criticism: such a context requires a high level of mutual trust and security before it can flourish at all. Without it, individual workers proceed with some degree of autism: falling victim to uncritically-accepted or 'orthodox' ways of doing research, to collective prejudice, or to their own private fantasies.

3. For similar reasons, the qualifications which it is desirable that the members should have do *not* look much like those commonly in force. They are of a highly general kind: the person should be clear-headed, possessed of a fair degree of critical intelligence, refuse to tolerate any kind of jargon or concealed nonsense, be able to give and take criticism in discussion without offence or alarm, and have sufficient positive enthusiasm for the enterprise in its own right. This does not, in my judgement, correlate much with degrees and academic qualifications in general, or with the expertise in the particular 'disciplines of research' (psychology, sociology, etc.) which often do little more than institutionalize logically misguided procedures and prejudices.

4. The research team as a whole must be trusted, within extremely broad limits, in terms of time, money and general procedure. This is because most educational research cannot sensibly be structured in short-term projects with very specific time-scales; because the kind, and amount, of expenditure is not generally predictable in advance; and because in short-term projects (of three years' duration, for example) those doing the work will spend most of their time finding their feet, making sure that some specific 'end-product' emerges, looking for the next job to go to, and so on. But the real point is that the intellectual aspects of educational research are such that those actually *doing* the work must be in a position to define its scope, determine its methodology, and organize the timing and expenditure. This whole business (what I have called the 'general procedure') is not something extrinsic to the research, to be decided beforehand by some professional committee or by some general consensus: *it is part of the research itself* (Wilson, J. 1972).

5. Finally, the research must not be affected at any stage or level by political or semi-political pressures. Research is concerned with truth and practical action guided by truth, not with accepting and acting out the predetermined views of politicians, teachers,

committees, or public opinion. What people want and think to be true or right is one thing: what they really need, and what is really true or right, something else. Prevailing opinions (which, any-way, change with changing educational and social fashions and climates) cannot be taken for granted: and this holds as much (or more) for positions involving 'values' as for those involving 'facts'. This relates to 1 and 4 above; and it is, I think, a failure of clarity and nerve in this respect that has castrated so much educational research (Wilson, J. 1979b).

Only a very naive person would expect those institutions and organizations which are concerned with the funding and arrange-ment of research either to grasp these points intellectually or to put them into practice: first, because the points only emerge with real clarity from a rather sophisticated philosophical (or, in a broad sense, 'methodological') enquiry, and very few of those who man and control the institutions have the relevant expertise; and second-ly, because there are in any case political or administrative pressures which prevent the kind of freedom and decentralization of power that is necessary. Whilst it is, I think, possible to criticize these bodies for not being rather more intellectually serious in trying to grasp what proper educational research is and rather more bold in actually advancing it, the attribution of blame is not very profitable here. The enterprise requires a degree of understanding and trust which is, generally speaking, simply not there.

Faced with this situation, we had two options. One was to 'play the system': I mean, to make whatever moves seemed necessary to get the research funded: canvassing the support of well-known academics and others, filling out the required forms in a way which would appeal to the relevant committees, softening up the opposi-tion by making and exploiting the right contacts, and so on. The other was to go it alone. We chose the latter for this particular exercise, chiefly because we envisaged a fairly small scale enterprise that would not need large sums of money, which (we hoped) could be conducted more or less anonymously, without the benefit of public relations or any kind of politics. Even if we had been immediately successful in obtaining funds, the time and effort spent on non-research activities required by 'the system' might be no less than the time and effort required actually to do the research work.

This is not, of course, to deny that the organized institutions have in principle a very important part to play: and some of us hope to use their services for further work, in this and other fields, of a more elaborate and expensive nature. But we all felt that it would be extremely interesting to operate *one* serious piece of research without reference to them, if only for the sake of a contrasted example: and our own topics seemed good candidates. It would at least offer a paradigm of research in an area of great practical importance which was totally freed from the usual conventional pressures. We have seen, since then, no reason to change this judgement.

Before describing how we proceeded after having made that decision, I ought to enlarge slightly on what we had already attempted; for this, in its own way, was as important as anything we did thereafter. Together with other people in the same seminars, committees, schools and so on, we had spent some time in discussing rather haphazardly the notions of discipline and ME, and experiencing its practical forms. As a result of this, we had already reached certain conclusions before starting the research or even identifying ourselves as researchers. These, though in some ways obvious, are worth listing:

a. We realized that we were *not* agreed, or not clear, about what ground words like 'discipline', 'well-disciplined', 'moral' etc. covered: that is, we were not entirely clear what we were talking about.

b. We suspected that there were a number of *different* things, marked by different words (e.g. 'discipline', 'obedience', 'control', 'organization' 'motivation', etc), which needed to be sorted out first: each or all of these might have been important topics for educational research, but unless we could distinguish them we could not show what kind of importance they had, nor conduct research on any of them properly.

c. We felt that, so far as practical discipline and ME in schools were concerned, both our actions and our reactions stemmed from some uncritically-accepted prejudice or ideology (usually of a tough- or tender-minded kind): that is, as regards both what we did with children and how we assessed what others did, we were not proceeding from any clear grasp of particular educational goods, but rather from what sorts of 'behaviour', or 'system', or 'style' happened to suit our own particular mental make-up. We also felt ourselves much influenced, either directly or reactively, by the prevailing educational fashions.

These conclusions, though negative, were an essential starting point. They correspond in most respects to a state of mind familiar to readers of the Socratic dialogues: the *aporia* or doubt which overtakes a person who thought he knew what piety (virtue, justice, etc.) was, and what ought to be done about it, but who on reflection realized that he did not know, and that his behaviour was not founded on any firm understanding.

At this point a kind of self-selection procedure operated to define the 'we' who engaged in research. Some people did not feel particularly enthusiastic about taking things further: thinking perhaps that it did not particularly matter whether or not we could establish what discipline or ME were and what ought to be done in practice; or perhaps that this task seemed alarming, or time-consuming, or impossible to carry out; or perhaps just that it was not their cup of tea. The criterion here is best described by 'the term 'seriousness'. These people were not 'serious' about this particular job; and there is no question of criticizing them here, not only because many of them were very busy people with other things to do besides research but also because we are not all called upon to be 'serious' about the same enterprises: educational research is, indeed, not everyone's cup of tea. Others however – that is, 'we' – felt that it was, for us, intellectually and psychologically intolerable to leave things as they were. Although we could not or ought not to spend all our time on it, we wanted to go further.

These people constituted what I have (rather grandly) called the 'research team', the members of which worked together on and off (mostly off), for some eight years (1972–80). We already knew each other fairly well, and soon appreciated the importance of those features listed earlier (trust, security in mutual criticism, and so on). Naturally the work brought us into intimate contact with each other, and relationships between some members of the group were very close. Some of the people concerned wished to give time to some form of 'group therapy', 'group dynamics', and so forth, but in general the initial seriousness about the *work* overrode what might otherwise have been threats to its advancement. It is, in fact, very difficult in the context of this kind of research to draw a clear line between the raising of personal issues (discussions of individuals' emotions and prejudices) which are useful for the work on the one hand and those which are either self-indulgent or based on undue optimism on the other. It is easy for any individual to *use* a working group of this kind to advance either the solution of his own problems or some general cause ('complete mutual honesty') for which the group is not originally intended and not adequately constructed. But we did our best: the reader must judge by the quality of the work which emerged rather than by any overall improvement in our mental health.

Anonymity

A word now on the question of anonymity, firstly as regards the research subjects. There are both theoretical and practical difficulties in trying to get a tolerably accurate picture of the concepts and principles which a person entertains. One such set of difficulties – only one, but it is important – can be removed by anonymity: certain rather obvious and often quite justifiable fears, mostly connected with authority, may be laid at rest; and also – something that surprised us rather more – certain desires, usually less justifiable, can be quashed. Thus both the person who feared that the headteacher, or the local educational authority, would affect his career adversely, and the person who desired to make some kind of name for himself by 'giving us the low-down' on a particular school, could be to some extent aborted. We learned quite soon to recognize the hunted or suspicious look in the eyes of the former, and the glint in those of the latter.

The disadvantages of anonymity are straightforward: our work cannot be checked 'on the ground' by other researchers, and *some* (not all) objections about the sample of subjects cannot be refuted without disclosing what is better hid. I do not think, however, that these disadvantages are of much importance. We are not making any overall empirical generalizations or attempting any overall statistic claims about opinions in our society (or any other) as a whole, such that the sample of individuals needs very careful inspection. All that we have to show, for our conclusions, is that the individuals who were investigated could not reasonably be considered as unique, in the sense that the conclusions were unlikely to apply anywhere else.

The anonymity of the researchers themselves raises more complicated questions, in that it relates to the whole business of how educational researchers should present themselves to schools, their honesty and credibility, and their moral standing in general. Our own case is here peculiar, if not unique, and its justification need not be taken as applying to educational research in general. The most obvious reason for anonymity was prudential: many of our team felt (understandably) that, if they were identified and proclaimed as 'doing research on discipline' ('ME'), then (a) the responses they got from the research subjects would be misleading, in the ways described above, and (b) their own position in schools and elsewhere might be adversely affected. (Many of them were student-teachers or practising teachers, and might be distrusted by their colleagues and the authorities – perhaps even lose their jobs, or be disqualified for promotion.) There seemed, therefore, a *prima facie* case for anonymity both in doing the research, and in subsequently publishing it.

On the other hand, we were worried about subjecting the schools and individuals in question to any kind of *deception*. Would we not be acting somewhat in the role of undercover-men or spies, masquerading as ordinary teachers or student-teachers, but actually trying to dig down into areas which the research subjects would have kept hidden from any self-proclaimed outsider? We felt this to be a rather over-dramatized picture of the actual situation, for two main reasons. First, the role and interests of the team members were *not*, in fact, primarily connected with research: they were *teachers* or student-teachers, and had no thought of doing anything which was not consistent with their jobs. Secondly, it would have been impossible to say at any early stage 'We are conducting research on discipline and ME, for such-and-such a period, and our findings will eventually be published in such-and-such a form', simply because the work was not organized in that way. We did not know how long the work would take, whether it would be publishable at all, what evidence from what people we would want to take account of, or anything of that kind.

What then could we say, to avoid any question of deception? Arguably, we need have said nothing at all. Few schools or individuals would actively discourage, or want to prevent, their members of staff and student-teachers from observing what other people thought and from themselves thinking about it: that is, essentially, from 'doing research' in a broad sense of the phrase. It is, for instance, quite usual for student-teachers to write up various features of the schools in which they do their practice teaching: and practising teachers can hardly avoid some discussion and promulgation of what they observe and think, just as they can hardly avoid some observing and thinking. Questions of loyalty to the institution, or of breaking some (usually tacit) convention of privacy and silence vis-à-vis the outside world, would normally arise only by the *publication* of what the institution wanted to keep hidden, in such a way that it reflected badly on the institution concerned. But that is covered by the anonymity of the research subjects: it is, in fact, quite impossible for the reader to make any identification either of particular schools or particular individuals. Nevertheless, most of us felt that this was not quite good enough, that if we had *some* intention of investigating a particular area, then *something* ought to be said about it, at least if we were asked. We were caught, in fact, between the needs (i) to be honest about our intentions in the sense of not *concealing* them, and (ii) to be honest in the sense of not *misrepresenting* them (as we would if, for instance, we represented ourselves as paid-up professional researchers who intended to publish certain facts in certain forms).

What we did, in fact, was to be as honest as we could and to give as full an explanation as was possible: not making too formal a proclamation in advance, but not refusing to state our general interest. Thus a team member might say, before talking to one of his colleagues or pupils, something like 'I'm extremely interested in your views on discipline', adding, 'in fact it might help to make up a book one day, though of course not with your name or the name of your school mentioned'. He would then explain that he was one of a number of people who had a collective interest in the topic, and hoped – only hoped – that the material they collected would eventually be publishable, but that they did not represent any institution, and that the research was not 'official' or funded by anyone. He might also have to state firmly – something which worried some respondents – that he was not in any way representing the press or other mass media, and that there was no question of any individual or school being subjected to 'trial by television'. On the whole, I think we erred here on the side of creating too formal an impression of organized research: over-anxious not to deceive anyone, we may have suggested a much more coherent, orthodox and 'official' type of project than was actually the case. In fact, since many of us did actually take part in many informal conversations and discussions of these and other educational topics, it was very difficult in some cases to say whether a particular conversation was 'research material' or not: but if there seemed any chance at all that it might be, we said our piece in advance. Certainly no one has been lulled into a false sense of security: in respect of all the material actually used, every respondent was warned adequately. It is still possible, I suppose, that an unusually suspicious or distrustful person might regard this anonymity as no more than a mask for incompetent or improperly conducted research, or even, perhaps, for the mere fabrication or invention of evidence. That suggestion could, of course, be made about a good deal of educational research which also conceals (to a greater or lesser extent) various identities and sources of information behind the veil of anonymity, usually for reasons similar to our own – to avoid making certain institutions or individuals 'look bad', and to obtain less biassed responses from them. I do not see how any suggestions of this sort could be thoroughly refuted, short of unveiling all the facts. That is, of course, quite possible in the natural sciences, since the notion of public relations does not apply to atoms or even rats, nor are their responses biassed. But for human beings the price of uncovering privacy is often too high to pay.

We have taken, in fact, an extremely firm stand on this from the very beginning of our work. Partly because some subjects showed extreme alarm at even the faintest possibility of disclosure, and partly because we felt it proper to make our precautions as effective as possible, we agreed (and told the subjects) not only to keep the names of individuals and institutions under a veil, but actually to destroy the notes, tape-recordings, interview sheets, tables and so forth after they had been translated into the substance of this book: this, in fact, we have recently done. This may itself seem slightly paranoid; but there have actually been cases, both here and overseas, in which such data have been illegitimately – even illegally – plundered and used for purposes of publicity and gossip. At a time when the employability (let alone the personal feelings) of teachers and student-teachers is very much at risk, we felt it better to take no chances.

Although I have discussed this topic at some length, I should maintain that whatever merits this book has ought not, as we see it, to be severely impaired by the rightness or wrongness of our judgements about anonymity. Even if the empirical details of what we claim to have done cannot themselves be verified, nevertheless the substance of what we say can be verified by anyone who cares to take the trouble. The study can be replicated, in the sense that the same sorts of conclusions would (we believe) be reached by any researchers who asked similar questions and set about answering them in similar ways. Much of what we say is, in any case, a matter of conceptual or phenomenological analysis: even the empirical side is more a matter of detailed description (to put it at its lowest) of how *some* teachers, parents, pupils, etc. might think and act about discipline and ME. If some reader were to regard it as a piece of insightful fiction, the insights would still be there. Whilst of course it is, in reality, also an attempt to establish some empirical truths or 'facts', we are sincere in saying, at least, that readers will derive *most* benefit from it by way of a general sophistication of their thinking, and not – or not only, and certainly not primarily – by way of collecting some hard pebbles of 'scientific' knowledge. It is, as I have said, an *initial* project only: an attempt to start educational research off on the right foot, when it has been hopping about for so long on the wrong one.

CHAPTER TWO
Methodology

I turn now to some rather more strictly academic considerations about our research methodology, which flow from some points about educational research in general: points in themselves perhaps fairly obvious, but certainly constantly neglected in practice. First, a rough distinction may be drawn between those research topics which necessitate the teacher and/or the learner having to get clear about certain concepts, and those which do not. We may illustrate this by taking obvious cases on either side. If (i) our topic were 'learning mathematics' or 'doing science', obviously both teachers and learners would have to know what mathematics or science *were*: they would have to possess the concepts which we mark by 'mathematics' and 'science', together with a good many other concepts which constituted those disciplines. If (ii) our topic were, say, 'the heating of school buildings', then it might not matter much (or at all) whether or not teachers and pupils knew anything about heating, or even knew what heating was (what 'heating' meant): we could find out how to get a reasonable air-temperature in schools, without too much expense or fire-risk, which the teachers and pupils could simply profit from whilst remaining in total ignorance of these facts.

Nearly all educational topics – that is, topics which have some fairly direct connection with *learning* – do, in fact, fall into the former category; and for this reason it is quite hard to think of clear cases which fall into the latter. For instance, a topic enshrined in the phrase 'fire precautions' might partly consist of research about non-inflammable materials, automatic sprinklers and so on, in other words, 'precautions' which would operate quite independently of anyone's *understanding* them. Naturally, it would also include things like fire drill, the use of emergency exits, etc. which clearly involve understanding. In fact, without *any* kind of understanding something may always go wrong even with the 'brute' cases in class (ii): thus if nobody on the spot actually *knew* that the automatic sprinklers were sprinklers, they might tear them down and use them as scrap metal.

A good deal depends here on how we ourselves interpret particular research titles. Because of certain pressures on researchers, often of a political or semi-political kind, there is a regrettable tendency to misinterpret them in such a way as to overlook the fact that they fall into class (i) rather than class (ii). To use an example more fully discussed elsewhere (Wilson, J. 1972), anyone who took the title 'racial prejudice' seriously – that is, who was committed to research on *racial prejudice* rather than something else – would rapidly come to see that the notion marked by 'prejudice' involved certain *beliefs* (roughly, beliefs generated by emotion rather than evidence), as well as certain overt behaviour. He would need, consequently, to guide his researches towards finding out how people thought and felt about other races, as well as how these thoughts and feelings emerged in behaviour. But if all we are really interested in is actually preventing certain admittedly objectionable *events* – inter-racial assassination, or whatever – then we need only find effective methods of prevention, and not necessarily educational methods. The job might best be done by advertising, or the use of drugs, or some form of conditioning. Here we need not (though we may) bother to investigate concepts and beliefs at all, though of course our research could not then be correctly entitled 'racial *prejudice*'.

Does it matter if we misinterpret research titles in this way? The strict answer is that we cannot tell whether it does or not until we have interpreted them correctly: for only grasping a correct interpretation will tell us whether that interpretation represents something important, something which (because we have uncritically accepted our own misinterpretation) we shall have paid no attention to. Thus if we interpret 'racial prejudice' simply in terms of certain overt behaviour, we shall have omitted to find out anything of how people think and feel about other races; or, to put it another way, unless we make sense of the 'behaviour' by checking on the beliefs and feelings that are enshrined in it, we shall be left simply with the 'brute' phenomena of certain physical movements. It is, in fact, clear enough in almost all cases that, if we ride rough-shod over the normal language of our research titles, we are likely to omit a good deal that is important: perhaps particularly those things which are characteristically human.

'Discipline' is a case in point. For reasons which we shall make fully clear later (Chapter 3) the existence of anything properly to be described under this title involves the possession of certain concepts and the deliberate following of certain rules. Ants, formal gardens, or carefully designed irrigation canals are not well-disciplined except in a metaphorical sense: the term properly applies only to *people* and groups of people, and it applies to people not just *qua* bodies or physical creatures but *qua* rational creatures; that is, creatures who can possess concepts and follow rules. If this is so, then clearly the essence of research into discipline will be to determine what these concepts and rules are, and to what extent the relevant people do actually possess and follow them; together, of course, with the reasons why they do or do not, and what can in practice be done to help them.

We need, of course, to show – and shall show later – that this is not, as people sometimes say, 'just a linguistic point', and does not rest on some philosophical doctrine about the importance of 'normal usage' or 'ordinary language'. An initial approach to this might be to see whether there were other words in other languages besides English which covered the same ground; if there were, that might at least suggest that there was some important and widespread human interest here, which these words were used to mark – that we had not, so to speak, just happened upon some quirk peculiar to contemporary English. But to be really safe, stronger arguments are required. We have to elaborate the *concept* or range of meaning marked by 'discipline' and show that this concept is logically required by human beings in general.

By 'logically required' I do not mean (a) that every human being must in fact have a clear grasp of the concept, but equally I do not intend (b) some kind of questionable 'value-judgement', as it is sometimes called, to the effect that human beings just ought, in our opinion, to entertain and value the concept. I mean that if we engage in anything which can be recognized as human life, the concept can be seen to be necessary and important. For example, one could not conceive of human beings without some kind of body, or of it not being important to keep that body in whatever may be thought to be a proper state: the concepts marked by 'body' and 'health' will therefore be inevitable. Similarly there could not be such things as social groups whose members communicated with each other unless there were some practice of truth-telling and keeping contracts: so that these concepts, marked perhaps by 'telling the truth' or 'keeping one's word', will have an inalienable importance for any society, whatever 'value-judgements' anyone may make and whether or not the members of that society are clear about the concepts and their importance. These things are, as it were, *given*: we are *landed* with them, whether we like it or not. Only a naive relativism, which exercises an undue influence in educational theory and practice, prevents us from grasping these rather obvious points. In fact, it is often not necessary to use such strong arguments. In educational research, certain things are given in a more detailed or specific way than that in which they are given for men in general. It is crucially important, however, to see that *what* is thus given must not come from a deferential acceptance of existing states of affairs that could well be otherwise – from the pressures of politics, public opinion, a particular way of running schools in our society, or whatever. For such things we can, and often ought, to change. What we cannot change are the concepts given to us *by the enterprise of education itself*. Thus if someone suggested that we did not need to bother about concepts marked by, say, 'teaching' and 'learning' in any educational research, we should find it hard to understand him; perhaps there is something he is interested in, but he is certainly not interested in *education*. So it is with discipline. As long as we are concerned with teaching and learning, or with any institution in which teaching and learning are supposed to go on (whether or not we call this a 'school'), the concept marked by 'discipline' has, as we shall show, an inalienable relevance and importance.

This point has considerable practical force. For if the researcher, or anybody else, is to make any actual *use* of the research, much will depend on whether the research topic is tied in the way just described to inalienable, rather than disputable, goods. If we take as 'given' certain things which perhaps ought not to be given – the particular practices in our society, or current educational conventions and fashions – our research, however expertly conducted, will always be liable to a basic challenge. For example, researchers in Nazi Germany or Communist China might take it as given that children should be taught in certain ways and learn certain things, and spell out how this is to be achieved, and even *call* it 'moral education'; but, very obviously, the value of this work rests upon highly disputable ideologies, which (one might rather nastily say) only a very servile or corrupt researcher would want to follow. These are extreme examples, but the same point holds in our own and other more 'liberal' societies. If we simply *assume* that whatever is meant by 'breaking down the barriers of social class', 'integration', 'mixed ability', 'relevance to the modern world', and other such phrases – the list is endless – is desirable, we have omitted the most important part of our work. We are certainly not entitled to make any practical suggestions about how things can be improved, since we have not even examined the question of whether the attainment of these objectives is, in fact, an 'improvement'.

These two main points form the logical platform on which any serious research in this area must be based. To repeat, they are (1) that discipline and ME involve the possession of certain concepts and the following of certain rules, and (2) that they are of inalienable importance to education – not things whose 'value' can be intelligibly questioned. The first sets the style, as it were, of the research: the second shows that the research is worth doing.

We need now to say something about the methods and difficulties which are relevant to the empirical aspects of this sort of research, that is, research which involves finding out what concepts people possess and what rules they follow. There is one important guiding principle here: the principle that, though this is essentially a *different kind of enquiry* from research in the natural sciences or research along what might roughly be called 'behaviouristic' lines, nevertheless there are *equivalent standards of stringency*. It is perhaps the failure to grasp this point and explore it properly that accounts for much contemporary research which, while rightly showing some dissatisfaction with 'behaviouristic' methods, nevertheless is content with excessively vague standards and types of verification, sometimes optimistically described as 'illuminative'.

What we have to get rid of is the idea, still very powerful even in the minds of those who ostensibly reject it, that if our research is not 'scientific' ('objective', etc.) *in the way that* research in the natural sciences should be, then this must imply some falling-off in stringency and objectivity: that we simply do the best we can, in a rather nebulous or 'subjective' way, to make sense of our research topic. This idea is, unfortunately, reinforced by the continued use of a terminology which is perhaps (though there are doubts even about this) more appropriate to natural science, and of techniques which have long formed part of the orthodoxy of educational research. For instance, naive talk of 'data' or 'the facts' which we subsequently have to 'explain' commonly suggests too sharp a disjunction: in interpreting human thought and behaviour, what counts as 'a fact' is usually much more disputable than in natural science, and it is rarely possible to draw any clear line between 'observation' and 'explanation' – how one *identifies and describes* what is happening turns out to be almost the whole story. For similar reasons, statistical and other such techniques are only of immediate use when we can make this disjunction; otherwise, they have to wait until we have some agreed and established 'data' for there to be statistics *of*.

To take some near parallels, it is entirely clear that the understanding and research of the historian or the clinical psychologist are, in their own way, just as 'objective' or in a sense 'scientific' as those of the natural scientist. Notions like 'evidence', 'verification' and 'proof' still apply, so too do the ideas of 'prejudice' or 'bias'. These concepts simply have different criteria of application: we all know that a historian or a judge can be unbiased, that a physicist can be unbiased, and that what counts as bias in each case depends on the subject matter of the particular enquiry in which each is engaged. Again, we recognize in broad terms what it is for historians or psychiatrists to be 'in the grip of a theory', or for their 'value-judgements' to get in the way of their research; and contrariwise, we recognize the historian or psychiatrist who 'does justice' to his topic or subject. It is a matter of what *sort* of justice has to be done.

It will be asked whether there is, in educational research of this kind, any parallel to 'scientific method'; that is, presumably, certain well-established procedures of observation, experiment, repeatability, the testing of hypotheses, and so forth. In one sense there is such a parallel: there are techniques for finding out what people think and do, and one may (if the terms are not misleading) conduct 'experiments' on them, 'test' certain 'hypotheses' about them, and so forth. But in another sense there is not: and here, there is certainly an important difference between the two. The difference consists largely in the fact that research on human behaviour is in its infancy, and will remain so until we have at least sufficiently clear and agreed descriptions of 'the facts' to proceed to the further stage of theory. At present – there may be a parallel with the early stages of taxonomic botany or zoology – we do not even have clear categorizations and descriptions: this means, as I have already implied, that the essential work consists in categorizing and describing. For this work, there are no algorithmic rules and no cut-and-dried 'method'.

There is however what might be called a 'method' in a wider sense. It consists in matching descriptions to different aspects of the world – in our case, to what human beings say and do. We already use this method in our everyday lives (and in virtue of it know quite a lot about our neighbours), and it would be tempting to describe it as 'common sense', were it not that it requires a good deal of sophistication to use properly. The kind of sophistication in question takes two forms, which are connected with each other. First, we have to be linguistically or philosophically adept; that is, practised in trying out different descriptions on items of the world, in recognizing misfits and in identifying clear cases and borderline cases; in short, versatile and not content with anything short of exactitude. This is, of course, a well-recognized procedure in philosophy, and our failure to apply it to educational research has been disastrous. (The best exponent is J.L. Austin: see for instance Austin, J.L. 1961. Austin himself calls the process 'linguistic phenomenology' (ibid., p. 130).) Secondly, we have to shed any particular prejudices (and almost any theory counts as a prejudice here) to the effect that a phenomenon *must* be of a certain kind or described in a certain way: in this respect existing psychological or sociological theories and concepts are likely to be a positive hindrance. These two features are connected, because of course the ability to deploy the first depends on the second: unless we are reasonably free from partisan prejudice, we shall not be any good at trying out various descriptions and getting the right one.

Other problems of course also give some trouble in this area. There are, for instance, questions about the sincerity or self-deception of a person's replies – about how we are to establish what he 'really' thinks and feels, when his thought and feeling may vary from one context to another, and about the conceptual and empirical connections between his thought, feeling and action. I shall not enlarge on these here, partly because I have considered them elsewhere (Wilson, J. 1973), partly because they will emerge more clearly in those chapters which describe our research in greater detail, but chiefly because – as it turned out – there was sufficient conjunction of evidence for us to be in no serious doubt about our main findings, so that these particular problems did not in practice prove too troublesome.

Investigations into people's 'opinions', 'perceptions', 'views', 'judgements', etc. have characteristically failed to attend to three aspects of any such enquiry, which correspond to three inalienable features of it. The enquiry will necessarily be concerned with propositions whose general form is 'S (the subject or respondent) believes P (the subject's opinion, or belief, or the proposition which he entertains) about X (the subject matter which S is asked about)'. First, the description of X will be likely to mean different things to different Ss: thus if S is asked his views about, say, 'sex education', S1 may take this to mean instruction in biology, S2 assume that it implies some sort of moral exhortation, S3 some discussion of emotions and personal relationships, and so on. Secondly, what S says may be construed in many ways: as expressing a belief or judgement, a feeling or prejudice, an ideal or taboo, a fantasy, and many other things: a difficulty which goes beyond the already notorious variety both in (a) what S's actual words may mean, and (b) what S's speech-act may be. Much that an S says and (overtly) means as an opinion or judgement may in fact be nothing of the kind. Thirdly, it is naive to assume that the psyches of all (or perhaps of any) Ss are so monolithically constructed that there is some *one* thing which corresponds to 'what S thinks'. The point is not just that S may think one thing on one occasion and another on another: it is rather that we are forced to speak of tapping different *levels* of S's mind – levels whose operation may, indeed, correspond to different social or other contexts (one level surfacing in committees or other public contexts, for instance, another in privacy, and a third on the psychoanalyst's couch) but which exist independently of them.

Quite long conversations, under informal conditions, are required even to begin to get any clear results in the face of such difficulties. Much will depend, of course, on how sophisticated the enquirers are: thus if they themselves are clear about the subject matter (X), and able to explain it without ambiguity – or rather, to clarify it and distinguish it from ambiguities which the subject (S) may have in mind – a good deal can be achieved. The way in which S says what he says (tone of voice, style of speech, facial expressions, etc.) is also of obvious importance, particularly in determining the content of P: that is, what sort of thing he is *doing* when he 'says what he thinks' (judging, letting off steam, reinforcing his fantasies, and so forth). The work can perhaps be described as a sort of blend which involves both philosophical and psychiatric competence: this is a herculean task, and one which has received very little theoretical attention from researchers or methodologists.

Although we shall go into more detail later, it may now be helpful to formalize (if only in a very general way) the crucial questions which need to be answered. We assume – what will also need further discussion – that we have a reasonable sample of research subjects, referred to in the following questions as 'they' and 'them'. Given that, it seemed that we need to find out:

1. Did they have a clear understanding and firm grasp of the concepts marked by 'discipline' and 'ME'? If and in so far as they did not, then
   (a) What deficiencies were present?
   (b) What caused these deficiencies?
   (c) What could be done to remedy them?
2. Did they have a clear understanding and firm grasp of the necessity or practical importance of these concepts? If and in so far as they did not, then
   (a), (b) and (c) as above.
3. Did they actually put these concepts into practice in schools? If and in so far as they did not, then
   (a), (b) and (c) as above.

These questions are, as they stand, extremely general, and we could not hope to answer some of them (certainly not 3); but it is at least clear that they have to be asked in that order. It is a necessary, but not sufficient, condition of grasping the importance of a concept that a man has that concept: so we have to determine 1 before 2. Similarly it is a necessary, but not sufficient, condition of putting a concept into practice both that a man has the concept and that he thinks it important: that is, 1 and 2 must come before 3.

I do not deny the possibility, at least, of some logical overlap between 2 and 3 along lines much discussed by moral philosophers. Thus it might be argued that (2) to 'think something important' at least implies that the person *would* (3) 'put it into practice' if he could: otherwise, we might want to say, he cannot 'really' ('sincerely' etc.) think it important. I myself deny this, so far as the normal use of such phrases as 'think right', 'believe in', 'think important', etc. goes: but we can in any case avoid discussion of this problem by stipulating that 2 refers only to assent 'in principle' or 'in theory'; roughly, an assent which might sometimes or even often not be cashed out in their practical choices and behaviour (owing to some countervailing factor). In something like the same sense, a man might assent to the importance of health and the avoidance of smoking, yet still continue to smoke.

What possible answers – again in very general terms – were there to these questions? We were concerned with the reasons why discipline and ME were or were not properly understood and practised, and in preliminary discussion we made a rough classification of possible reasons. To state these boldly and naively, it might be:

(A) simply that not enough effort had been made by those directly concerned – teachers and pupils – to *understand* what discipline and ME were and why they were important: in other words, that the main weight of the answer lay in 1 and 2 above, and that (given such understanding) there were no major obstacles to (3) the actual practice of discipline and ME.

(B) that, even given such understanding, there were obstacles either

    (i)   of what might roughly be called an institutional or man-made kind (that the system of school management, for instance, or the law, or some other sort of man-made rule inhibited the realization of such understanding in practice), or

    (ii)   of a 'brute' kind, not (or not so directly) negotiable: for instance, that certain people had a low IQ, or came from a particular social class, or were not rich enough to attend boarding schools, and could not understand the concepts and what followed from them.

The distinction between (i) and (ii) above is, of course, not at all clearly drawn here, and, in fact, is better replaced by a much greater number of possible obstacles. But it perhaps suffices to introduce the next point.

We made some guesses ('hypotheses', if you prefer a grand word) about which of these categories might bear the main weight of the answers to our questions. Briefly, we guessed that the most important categories were (A) and (B) (i) – perhaps particularly (A) – and not (B) (ii). In other words, we considered the possibility that *if* (A) teachers, and subsequently pupils, together perhaps with those who might be said to be 'directly concerned' (e.g. parents), really had a clear grasp and understanding of discipline and ME, and *if* (B)(i) those responsible for schools at a higher level – local authorities, union leaders, civil servants, governors or whoever – were to alter certain rules in order to allow this understanding to operate, then there would *not*, (B) (ii), be very great difficulties in ensuring the actual practice of discipline and ME in schools generally: that is, it would *not* be the case that the home background of certain pupils, or their intellectual incompetence, or poverty, or social class, or anything of that kind necessarily prevented this practice.

We made some guesses about what inhibited the understanding which constituted category (A), and was obviously relevant to (B) (i) (since one possible set of reasons, at least, for the wrong kind of man-made rules made at higher levels was that the people at those levels themselves lacked the required understanding). Was it, for instance, simply that those concerned were too stupid? Or that they had not been *taught* properly about discipline and ME? Had they been *wrongly* taught? How far did their misapprehensions stem from their own fantasies, or from prevailing fashions in educational theory? Amid these and other possibilities we backed the hypothesis that no very high degree of *intellectual talent* was necessary for such understanding; that it was (putting it roughly) essentially a matter of common sense, or keeping one's head, or not being carried away by various kinds of prejudices. We predicted, therefore, that there would not be much correlation between the strictly intellectual or academic sophistication of the research subjects and their grasp of discipline and ME: in fact, perhaps unsurprisingly, this turned out to be an accurate prediction.

These two main guesses, here very briefly stated, largely determined the choice of research subjects. We were not, of course, aiming at an orthodox piece of educational research, involving the possibility of easy replication, random sampling, sophisticated statistical techniques, and so forth: this was, from the first, construed only as an *initial* piece of research on the topics of discipline and ME, undertaken in the hopeful anticipation that others – armed with the conceptual framework and general approach which we had developed – would be able to paint a picture which was both more exact and on a larger scale. Nevertheless (to repeat), we wanted to suggest the possibilities: (1) that it was primarily lack of *understanding*, together with the presence of inappropriate rules or absence of appropriate rules derived from this lack, which inhibited the effective practice of discipline and ME; *not*, or not only, 'brute' factors in teachers, pupils or society at large which could not be influenced easily by increased understanding; and (2) that the kind of understanding required was *not* available only to the highly intelligent or those who had enjoyed the benefit of some sophisticated form of education.

A difficulty endemic to this kind of enquiry is, of course, that the responses one gets are affected by any process of questioning, which may (though it does not always) sophisticate the respondent. Thus the respondent may come to *mean* something different by 'discipline' during the course of the conversation, particularly if the conversation is overtly devoted to the exploration of meaning (as in the extreme case of the Socratic dialogues). It might be held, though I think wrongly (since some people will resist to the death), that given enough time and talk everyone would end up with the same set of clearly defined concepts, since most concepts are marked by words whose rules were learned in very early years if subsequently forgotten or confused. Certainly different parts or levels of the mind make use of different sets of concepts: this is evident if only from the fact, amply verified in our own enquiry, that people would say different things in different moods and contexts.

In practice, however, it is not too hard to draw a rough and ready distinction. There is, on the one hand, a set of ideas and opinions sparked off by certain terms (in this case, 'discipline' and 'ME'): to get these, we conducted our conversations in an almost totally non-directive fashion, allowing the respondent to talk freely and without too many questions, certainly with no questions of a philosophical or meaning-guided kind. On the other hand, the respondent may reflect on these ideas and opinions and on the terms themselves for a brief period, in the company of another person (the researcher), and during this the concepts which he entertains are likely to become fairly clear. It might be thought that the amount of time required here is essentially arbitrary; with more time, more levels of the mind are uncovered and (perhaps) the nearer the person gets to the rules he originally learned. But in fact that is not a fair representation of the case. What seems to happen is that, *if* the person has somewhere in his mind a number of concepts about which he is reasonably clear, such clarity becomes apparent within a very few minutes (certainly well within the hour or two which was the average time for our conversations). If, on the other hand, he does not have these clear concepts anywhere near the surface of his mind, much more than an hour would be needed to create or recover them for him – indeed they may never be recoverable. The difference is analogous to (perhaps, in a way, the same as) that between the ordinary process of remembering something, which can usually be achieved at once or very rapidly under the ordinary stimulation of an enquirer, and some technical processes which aim to recover memories from the unconscious mind (such as psychoanalytic free association).

We conducted our inquiry then in two phases. Phase I was

non-directive: we invited, in effect, free association to take place in the thoughts and words of our respondents, sparked off by the terms 'discipline' and 'ME', though on occasion (as rarely as possible) we had to steer them back to relevancy if they rambled too far. That gave us some evidence on the initial or (as it were) uncontaminated mental states of the respondents. Phase II was concerned with trying to determine whether the relevant concepts *were there*, in the respondents' minds, and could be recovered by them under guidance without too much difficulty: whether, in brief, they could *come to see* – without any form of pressure or bullying – what the concepts really were and what followed from them.

Most people most of the time, and all people for a lot of the time, are dominated by what might be called, rather cumbrously, 'monolithic syllogisms' – action-guiding and opinion-guiding pictures or stereotypes of what counts as 'decent', 'honourable', etc. Without the benefit of prolonged psychoanalytic investigation (and even perhaps with that benefit) it is often difficult or impossible to determine the ultimate sources of a person's overt views. Thus one respondent said words to this effect, 'Well, there's got to be order in school, hasn't there? I mean, how could anyone get any work done otherwise? The pupils have got to be well behaved and obedient . . .', so that our researcher was about to classify him as one who had grasped the *point* of obedience and 'good behaviour', when he continued, 'Yes, and of course they should have their hair cut, and none of this pansy nonsense in their clothes', and a good deal more to the same effect. This suggested that he had a monolithic and unargued syllogism whose major premise was something like 'Pupils should be like *this*', i.e. some picture of respectability, almost an aesthetic ideal, which was taken for granted and not connected with any point or object at all (except, no doubt, that it had point for him in his own childhood).

At what point do rationalizations become reasons? For, like this respondent, many or all of us are in reality dominated by some such monolithic syllogism, but are able and willing to quote good ('utilitarian', if you like) reasons which do not really affect our behaviour, and may even enter our thinking only marginally. We took the (perhaps somewhat arbitrary) line that if the good reasons would actually operate, in our judgement, in at least *one* kind of behaviour – namely, their willingness to subscribe, by voting or public agreement, to some policy *for* those reasons – that was enough for our purposes, whatever other reasons might dominate their day-to-day behaviour. For instance, we might present the respondent with, 'But some people don't care about hair and dress: is there any reason other than what looks respectable?' If he said, 'Well, whatever you feel about it, you've got to keep long hair out of the way in a machine shop', or (on obedience), 'Well, I think kids should be respectful to their elders anyway: but even if you don't, they've got to obey in school if they're going to learn anything', then we felt that he at least appreciated the weight of those (utilitarian) reasons and would vote for a policy in accordance with them, whatever his motives for insisting on short hair or 'respect' for his own children in their daily lives.

All this, as may be imagined, took a good deal of time to tease out (nor do we claim anything like infallibility). But some sort of middle course has, for the making of public policy, to be steered between (a) the simple referendum-question whose answer will be largely uninformative because it gives the respondent no chance to say *why* he opts for something, or what it is *about* the thing which makes him opt for it, and (b) the idea of 'what they "really" want', which leaves the door open too wide for politicians and others to dictate what they take to be 'in their best interests'. We need rather to determine (c) what parents, teachers, etc. want, when given a chance to express it (and the reasons for it) at some length. *What* they opt for is so closely bound up with *why* they opt for it that (a) is absurd: yet it is virtually impossible to investigate (b) with any hope of complete success. We have to rely on (c) what reasons for their options they give and would stand by *if it came to a vote*.

At the end of our research on each topic, we found ourselves with information (in the form of tape-recordings, notes, or interview schedules) about the 'conceptual state', as it may be called, of about 1,200 subjects. These had been preselected in four broad categories with about 300 allocated to each:

A. Parents
B. Teachers
C. Pupils
D. Educational administrators and academics.

Some of these categories overlap. The most significant overlap, at least statistically, is between A and B: 31 per cent of the teachers were also parents. There is also an overlap between A and D, and between C and D: that is, some parents and some pupils came also into the category of those directly concerned with the control and organization of schools (as defined below). These overlaps, however, were too small to be of much importance (approximately 3 per cent and 1 per cent respectively), though they are also noted in the results.

The last category calls for more explanation. We wanted to get information about those people who, in a fairly broad sense, controlled or influenced the educational system from outside the school. The category is of course impossible to delimit precisely: but we tried to choose people whose views did, in fact, affect those rules, regulations or conventions which might be thought to impede or facilitate the practical operation of discipline in schools: in particular, rules about the power or scope teachers are allowed, the sanctions in force against undisciplined pupils, and so forth. They were sub-divided – again, with a good deal of unavoidable overlap – into three broad groups of about 100 each:

(i)   those in what might be called 'mainstream' positions of influence or power, in particular representatives of local or central governmental authority (the LEAs, DES, the Inspectorate etc.);

(ii) those with a fairly direct influence, such as school governors, members of the Schools Council and other quasi-official bodies, union officials, and so forth;

(iii) those with some indirect influence and in particular lecturers at Departments and Colleges of Education and educational researchers.

The assessment of overlap between these three categories is partly a matter of conceptual nicety; but we tried to avoid such overlap as much as possible, and consider that it cannot (on any reasonable criteria) be more than 10 per cent between any one category and any other.

We reduced the total number to a round 1,000, with 250 in each category (A–D), and the numbers in sub-categories D(i), D(ii) and D(iii) being 100, 50, and 100 respectively – our reason for the latter being that D(i) and (iii) seemed of greater potential interest. The remainder of the 'wasted' subjects were winnowed out on no other grounds than clarity or comprehensibility; that is, we removed those of whose opinions we were *least* certain. In fact, very few (I estimate about 30 or so) were strictly unusable in this sense: in all other cases the major features of their conceptual state showed as clearly as was possible in the course of a reasonably long conversation. We erred on the side of safety, however, and were thus enabled to deal with the amenable figure of 1,000 subjects in all.

I must now again emphasize the point that we were *not* primarily concerned with selecting and categorizing a sample (if we must continue to use this rather odious word) which was statistically 'representative' of anything, or of such a kind that certain advanced statistical procedures could be brought to bear on it. Such procedures, in any case, are primarily concerned with correlations and covariances: it is not at all clear that these *in themselves* are of great interest for educational research (the well-known example of a high correlation between height and university entrance springs to mind). In educational research we want to know the *causes* of success and failure: and here the establishment of correlations is not only of little use, but may be positively misleading. To defend them as a way of directing the researcher to possible causes will not do, not just because that would be an extremely long-winded and laborious method of direction but because causation in human behaviour does not fit this pattern. We have, as has already been explained, to determine the *concepts, intentions and values* of the subjects.

Hence there were two general criteria by which we selected our subjects.

(1) The first, evidently necessary, was easy availability. By this I mean not just that the people in question were approachable (by a questionnaire, for instance), but that they were sufficiently approachable to be willing and able to take part in a reasonably long conversation ('depth interview', if the jargon is preferred) under informal conditions. We had to be careful here in order to avoid a process of self-selection, since naturally talkative or loquacious people might seem easier subjects. We did not, therefore, choose only the least busy or those most anxious to air their views. In effect, we selected (subject to the second general criterion discussed below) those subjects with whom we had already struck up some acquaintance by other methods; not, I hasten to add, a false acquaintance developed simply in order to extract information from them later, but a genuine acquaintance based on the fact that the subjects already related to us for some other reason.

No doubt questions might be asked (certainly we asked them) about whether this loaded the dice in favour of some subjects; for instance, whether the team members were more naturally acquainted with subjects of a certain type or conceptual style. It seems impossible either to prove or disprove this. Certainly, so far as their views on discipline were concerned, it was striking that these views were often very *different* from those of the team members. In any case, we felt that the advantages of this procedure more than outweighed any possible defects; in particular, we had the chance of finding out what they *really* believed. For with any kind of questionnaire, formal interview, or other method in which conversation does not flow naturally, beliefs are likely to be produced by some *persona* rather than by the person himself: in some more or less subtle sense, the man says what he expects himself, or thinks he is expected by others, to say – or perhaps the opposite; but in any case, not what he really thinks.

We grant, or course, that there are problems about what a man 'really thinks'. Men will think one thing at one time and in one context and another thing at other times and in other situations. Nevertheless, most men who have any firm thoughts or beliefs at all show a certain consistency (if they did not, they would tend towards insanity), and we tried to check our procedure by not being content with a single conversation. We asked similar questions at different times and in different contexts; we found, in fact, that with certain obvious exceptions – for instance, when a teacher's headmaster was listening – the subjects' views were consistent enough. A few, who seemed to have either no views and beliefs at all or else hopelessly inconsistent ones, were 'wasted' among the 200 rejects.

(2) The second general criterion, really a set of multiple criteria, was the set of factors which we guessed *might* shed some light on the causes of subjects' conceptual state. We decided to take two groups of criteria (I and II below). The first group (I) was to consist of four items which could be established without much difficulty:

I.

(a) *Age*: this was established precisely in nearly all cases, though in some older age-groups we were content with accuracy within a year or two. On the hunch (surprisingly justified in the results) that quite young children, if properly approached, might be sufficiently clear-headed about discipline to merit attention, we grouped the ages thus:

  10–13
  14–18
  19–25
  25–40
  40–50
  50 and over

(b) *Sex*: we guessed that, in most age-ranges, some notions (for instance, that of obedience to authority) would be clearer in the minds of women rather than of men. This was a stupid guess, and we are much to blame for arguing from (perhaps correct) generalizations to the effect that most women are more conscientious, obedient, deferential, etc. to the suggestion, which does not at all follow, that they are more likely to grasp the notion of authority and the importance of (impersonal) deference to it. The results prove the guess to be wholly misguided.

(c) *Type of school:* I mean here the sort of school with which the subject was chiefly or uniquely associated. In the case of groups B and C (teachers and pupils) this presented no problems. In group A, some parents had children at more than one school: in D, some 'administrators and others' had connections with more than one school, whilst others had no particular connection with any. We ventured on no hypothesis here.

(d) *Social class:* we thought some interesting results might emerge if we used a quasi-aesthetic criterion of social class (not the boringly common criterion of occupation or economic rating) in terms of 'style of life'. We induced this from such features as accent, linguistic usage, preferred activities and tastes. Though, of course, a much longer account could be given (indeed a whole book could be written about the respective merits of various concepts of social class) we were able to agree in practice on allocations to two broad classes for which we borrowed the well-known terms 'U' and 'non-U'. We did, however, allow considerably more latitude for inclusion in the 'U' class than the somewhat stringent and sometimes obsolescent indicators used by the originators of these terms. Roughly, 'U' would include those within the life-styles of the upper and upper-middle class, 'non-U' the remainder. We ventured the tentative guess here that class would *not* be a good indicator.

Nobody in his senses would, of course, suppose that any of these criteria would *in themselves* constitute causes; nevertheless we felt that, taken in conjunction with others, they might shed some illumination on the general scene. Our second group of criteria was geared more directly to possible causal factors. We guessed that four things, at least, might be relevant in the case of discipline: (e) whether the subject had been dazed or corrupted by some aspects of recent 'educational theory', (f) whether he/she had ever held a position of responsibility, in the sense of having to control and operate a task-like situation in whch discipline was palpably essential, (g) whether he/she could fairly be described as 'tough-' rather than 'tender-minded', and, (h) whether he/she had a good sense of intellectual relevance and was able to take discussion seriously.

These formed group II of our criteria, as follows:

(e) *Educational theory*: we had to restrict this pretty severely, since almost everybody might be said to have been influenced by the general climate of educational opinion over the last few decades. The criterion could only be effectively applied to teachers, 'educationalists' and some parents. In the strongest cases we were able to identify actual books read or courses taken (most obviously, in teacher-education): in the weakest, at least the idea that 'they' (*sc.* 'the educational authorities') believed and practised such-and-such. (Thus most parents had at least a fairly clear idea that there was a new 'line' in schools nowadays, 'different from when we were children'.) In applying this criterion we tried to gauge, however roughly, both (i) how much the subject had been *exposed* to such 'theory', and (ii) how far it had *affected* him either positively or negatively. All this is of course very general: we doubted whether it was a basic cause, but felt that it might be at least contributory or reinforcing.

(f) *Responsibility*: our guess was that those who held (or had held) genuine responsibility – who had to 'carry the can', in the old army phrase – for groups of people in task-like or similar situations would have perceived the nature and importance of discipline more readily than others. No particular brilliance is required for this rather obvious guess, which unsurprisingly turned out to be right. Positions of responsibility, in this sense, included such things as being the captain of a team, in charge of a school outing, foreman, and so on.

(g) *Tough-minded*: our guess was that such people would at least be able to appreciate the necessity of discipline more than the tender-minded. These terms may remind the reader of dimensions used by professional psychologists, but here we intend them in a fairly common-sense way. 'Tough-minded' covers much the same area as 'practical', 'realistic', 'having common sense': 'tender minded' as 'sympathetic', 'soft-hearted', 'kindly'. Naturally we could only gain a general impression, but we nearly always tried (and were able) to mark different subjects as 'tough-' or 'tender-minded' *before* finding out how they conceived or valued discipline.

(h) *Autism*: our guess was that intellectually 'autistic' people, in the sense about to be described, would be less likely than others ('serious' people) to grasp the relevant points and concepts. 'Autism' was judged by (a) the ability and willingness to *listen* to questions or remarks, and (b) to *reply relevantly* to them; also (c) the ability to profit intellectually by a discussion. It seemed to us that (a) and (b) were more useful criteria than any more formal measurement such as an IQ test; we found, in fact, that in those of our subjects whose IQs we were able to determine by recognized tests (about 35 per cent) autism and seriousness in this sense correlated very poorly with low and high IQ. We used (c) as an additional indicator, since any effective conversation of the kind we used *could* always sophisticate the subject's conceptual state as it proceeded: this could be so even if (perhaps particularly if) the researcher conducted it, as we did, in either a non-directive or a Socratic manner; the subject begins to recognize distinctions he had not faced before, and so on. So we tried to turn this systematic defeat to good account and found it, in fact, a very important indicator.

Of these, (e), (f) and (g) did not seem particularly relevant to moral education and were used only for discipline (see p.107). Briefly, we felt that: (e) modern 'educational theory' would not have corrupted concepts of moral education, as it might have corrupted the concept of discipline; (f) whilst holding or having held positions of responsibility would clearly bear directly on an understanding of discipline, there was no similar (or no obviously similar) connection between responsibiity and moral education; (g) a proper grasp of moral education did not *prima facie* connect with being 'tough-' or 'tender-minded'. It seemed to us, therefore, foolish to make any guesses about correlations here: moral education was a more complicated notion than discipline, so that we needed to spend more time simply in finding out how people thought and less in advancing hypotheses prematurely.

Part Two

CHAPTER THREE
Understanding Discipline

Research into discipline offers us an extremely good example of some of the points made in previous chapters; and in particular, the need to get completely clear about the concepts involved, about what is *meant by* 'discipline' or 'well-disc iplined'. The example is a good one (a) because it rapidly becomes clear just how far conceptual clarity changes the kind of empirical research needed and (b) because the actual concept involved is (in my judgement) tolerably clear, and does not require a very lengthy philosophical analysis. This latter is, of course, disputable: and it is important that we spend sufficient time and trouble in getting things straight.

The Concepts

One broad or overall distinction at least must be enforced between whatever may be meant by pupils being well-disciplined on the one hand and various notions of the pupils being well-controlled, well-ordered, organized, or trouble-free on the other. Consider first the notion of a group of people or an institution being well-organized for a particular purpose. One can have a well-organized classroom, or army, or operating theatre, or youth camp: this has to do with the arrangements, perhaps even more specifically with what one might call the administrative arrangements, which facilitate the purpose. A youth camp is badly organized if the latrines are too far away (or too near), an operating theatre if it is not arranged that the assistant with the scalpel stands near enough to the surgeon, and a classroom if the desks do not give the children a clear view of the blackboard. To describe all this under the heading 'discipline' is palpably absurd. Now consider the notion of being trouble-free, or in a broad sense 'controlled'. We get trouble-free prisoners by putting them in chains, trouble-free children by slipping them tranquillizers, trouble-free surgical assistants, perhaps by paying them enough for them not to worry about their mortgages during the operation. Again, this has nothing specifically to do with discipline. And we could run similar arguments with other notions applicable to groups of people, for example, 'having high morale', 'enthusiastic', 'interested' and so on.

'Accepting rules' is much nearer the target, because it brings in the notion of obedience. When we talk about the discipline of (say) an army being good, we are not talking about whether its administrative arrangements are good, or whether the soldiers are trouble-free and quiescent, or whether their morale and enthusiasm are high – though all these may, contingently, affect discipline or reflect it. We are talking about whether they obey the rules. Perhaps something more than that, however: whether they can be relied on to obey the rules. Suppose we have soldiers who do obey the rules, only they do so rather slothfully and mutter curses under their breath and so on. Well, that is better than not obeying them, and certainly they are better-disciplined than soldiers who conduct wildly enthusiastic charges against the enemy on their own initiative. But we might think that their discipline was a bit suspect, or 'about to crack', or 'slack' or something like that. We are not just concerned with their overt obedience, but with some kind of disposition to obey.

Can we sharpen up the vagueness of 'some kind of disposition to obey'? First, of course, the well-disciplined soldier will not obey just anyone – he will obey the established authority (his commanders or military regulations); naturally there can sometimes be a question about what or who is the established authority. More difficult but crucial is whether he must have certain reasons for his obedience. Granted that he obeys consistently and obeys the established authorities, does it matter why he obeys? He must, of course, obey for some kind of reason and in some degree of consciousness. If, for instance, he was just reacting to a set of post-hypnotic commands, that would not suffice to call him 'well-disciplined', and indeed we might wonder whether to allow this as a fully-fledged case of obeying (it is rather more like animals obeying). But what kind of reasons must he use?

Suppose a Roman legion obeys Caesar consistently, but when Pompey takes it over the troops immediately grow slack and perhaps mutinous. We investigate and find that they obeyed Caesar because of his personal charm, not because he was the legitimate general: Pompey is also legitimate but charmless. Were they well-disciplined under Caesar? A science class is well-disciplined when in the hands of Mr X because they admire him and of Miss Y because they are in love with her, but disobedient with Mr Z because they hate him. Is the science class a well-disciplined class? Are they well-disciplined even with Mr X and Miss Y?

In a loose sort of way we call people 'well-disciplined' (or 'just', or 'kind', or all sorts of things) when their overt behaviour – so long as it has some sort of reason – is of a certain kind, but really the well-disciplined (just, kind etc.) person has to have a particular type of reason. In the case of discipline, the point would be that the person must obey the rules because they are authoritative. This is importantly different from obeying them because they happen to issue from an admired source. It is also importantly different from obeying them because they are good rules, or sensible rules, or rules required for the purposes of the institution – a feature of rules constantly stressed in the literature but irrelevant to the particular notion of discipline.

There is clearly a particular concept at stake here: roughly, the notion of obedience to established and *legitimate authorities as such*. One could say a very great deal about the practical importance of grasping this notion and making it part of one's life and behaviour. Indeed, it is difficult to see how, without this, any institution or society can do more than rely upon the *ad hoc* variety of bribes or threats that might get things done – Mr X's charm, Miss Y's beautiful appearance, payment for doing good homework, electric shocks, or whatever else we may wish to deploy. But quite apart from any question of the inefficiency or fragility of such pressures, to omit the notion of discipline in this sense is to omit a whole swathe of concepts (authority, punishment, contract, law and so on) which are logically inevitable for rational creatures.

What is it, though, to accept rules as 'authoritative'? What is it to obey something or somebody as a source of authority rather than just a source of power? We have somehow to tread a middle way between two ideas, neither of which coextend with the idea of discipline, which I shall call 'total consent' and 'submission to power'. Some examples:
1. Roman soldiers were (sometimes) well-disciplined if anyone ever was. But it would be grotesque to say that they had always given anything like free or total consent to their authorities, or had in some way freely contracted to abide by the rules. Many of them had been automatically forced, conned, lured or press-ganged

into service. Their good discipline plainly did not depend on a totally free acceptance, nor on their acceptance of the rules, commanders, campaigns, or anything else as necessarily good or desirable.

2. On the other hand, we cannot regard their behaviour – at those times when, and to the extent that, such behaviour was well-disciplined – as in any simple or direct way forced. They were not well-disciplined when their centurions had to cudgel them in order to get them to perform various tasks; my behaviour is not well-disciplined if I advance only because there is a sword at my back. Such behaviour may be in accordance with the rules in force, but my reason for so behaving is not to obey the rules. My thought is not 'I will advance, or else I shall have failed in my duty', but 'I will advance or else I shall get stabbed'.

To accept rules as authoritative, in the sense required for discipline, consists partly in accepting them as reasons for action. This is verified by whether, in the practical situations involved, the motivating thought is something like 'It's a rule' rather than anything else, for example, 'It's a good idea', 'I shall suffer if I don't obey', 'I like doing this sort of thing', etc. Whether this is in fact what I have called the 'motivating thought' can, at least in principle, be established by setting up enough controlled situations in which the irrelevant variables do not apply: we see how the subject thinks and acts when it is a bad rule, when he will not suffer for disobedience, and so on.

Discipline is concerned with the consistency and strength of those on-the-spot acceptances or cases of obedience to authority. This of course involves or presumes his overall acceptance of the authority as such, but it does not involve any question about why he accepts it. There may be all kinds of reasons why a person accepts or submits to a source of power. I may do this in something like total freedom, as perhaps when I decide to learn French and put myself in the hands of a French teacher. Or, more commonly, I may think that the existing political authorities, rotten though they are, represent the only practically desirable alternative at the present time, and so consent to their rules. Or I may simply find myself (perhaps more commonly still) in a situation where I have no immediate means of escape from the authorities or powers-that-be and opt to 'play their game' either because it is the best I can do for myself or because of mere inertia. Many other possibilities exist. The analogy with games, weak at some points, is here strong: why a person plays in the first place (and his general outlook on the game as a whole) is one thing, his detailed obedience to the rules as such, another.

Of course not all these rules are of the same kind, or stem from the same authority. A lot here turns on the subject of which 'well-disciplined' is predicated. Thus we conceive of a soldier, for the most part, as one who obeys the orders of others, these orders being represented in a fairly concrete form; that is, so long as he does what his superiors tell him, and obeys regulations laid down in some manual or rule-book, he is well-disciplined. It is not required that he should, on his own initiative, improve his marksmanship or map-reading – that (for a soldier) shows him to be keener or more dedicated, but not better-disciplined. A soldier's duty begins and ends with obedience to others. A well-disciplined chess player or athlete or swordsman, on the other hand, obeys rules inherent in his craft; such people are not just occupiers of roles, but also craftsmen. The chess player restrains his eagerness in deference to principles concerned with building up an adequate defence before attacking, the athlete paces himself rather than just running flat out and so on.

Pace the Latin derivation, it is today a little odd to use 'well-disciplined' even in such cases, just as it is odd to talk of someone as 'well-disciplined' in his moral relationships with other people. Perhaps this is because 'discipline' is most at home when closely connected with fairly clear cut social rules and situations – in an army, in an operating theatre, in a class-room, on a ship. The demands we make under 'discipline' seem pretty down-to-earth; thus we may say of a citizen who pays his taxes, keeps the peace, etc., that he is law-abiding, but not that he is well-disciplined. Now put him in ancient Sparta, where his life is much more a matter of quasi-military obligation, and the word becomes more natural. Most natural of all is its use not of an individual, but of a group: it is not, or certainly not primarily, Smith minor or Private Jones or Amompharetus who are well-disciplined, but the Lower Fifth, the Second Battalion and the Spartan army. Individuals are more likely to be described as simply 'disobedient'.

This does not imply, of course, anything about the constitutional basis (as one might call it) of the group. Roles, tasks, and duties may be allotted democratically – I mean, as a result of discussion and majority vote – or by a dictator. Discipline prevails when these duties are carried out in obedience to the rules; constitutional questions about who makes the rules, what methods there are of changing them, etc. are here irrelevant. It is perhaps a contingent fact that social groups who operate democratically create fewer contexts in which it is appropriate to speak of 'discipline' than do less democratic groups: that is, fewer contexts in which there are those less quasi-military obligations that make the word natural. For example, a ship's company which had a democratic constitution, on which everyone participated in decision-making, would in practice be more suited to a pleasure cruise than a battle; and we should not speak so easily of 'discipline' on a pleasure cruise. But it would be possible for a ship or a fleet to change its constitution in the direction of democracy, at least to some degree, and still to operate in contexts where 'discipline' is relevant; that is, of course, by continuing to allot rules and tasks in a military style.

We can go further on these lines with the notions of 'task' and 'authority'. For 'discipline', 'well-disciplined', etc. to be in place, the task has to be a fairly specific or practical one. It is not a matter of discipline whether I, as a Christian, obey the authority of priest or scriptures in such matters as forgiving my enemies, loving my neighbour, and so on; on the other hand, it would be so if as a monk I obey or disobey more specific instructions, emanating from the abbot or the rules of my order. Similarly revolutionaries may be praised for ordering their lives according to the precepts of, say, Marx, but they are only praised for being well-disciplined in so far as they obey the orders of the revolutionary leader or committee. Being, in general, a good Christian or a good Marxist is not a task in the required sense.

But equally the task must be specific to the authority and the group – not just any obedience to accepted authority will do. A local policeman may often issue commands to the citizens in his neighbourhood but the citizens' obedience is not a case of good discipline in the way that the obedience of the policeman's subordinates in the police force would be. The citizens are under the policeman's authority but not, one might say, under his discipline. So too a teacher *qua* adult may give orders to children; but whether or not such orders can be regarded as authoritative, obedience to them is only a matter of discipline if the children are a working group under his particular authority for a particular purpose – if, that is, he gives his orders *qua* the teacher of a particular class of pupils or at least *qua* a teacher in the school of which they are members.

Obviously a group can be well-disciplined in respect of one authority and badly-disciplined in respect of another; for instance, the members of a revolutionary organization. Similarly, pupils' behaviour may be guided by the authority of their peer group or gang, or even perhaps of the school bully, rather than that of the teacher. We should often have difficulty in deciding whether we could sensibly talk of 'authority' here, rather than just 'power' or 'influence'. Clearly authority requires something in the way of formal recognition or acceptance (legitimization) and has to be to some degree institutionalized. But it is plain that two or more potential authorities might compete for obedience, even within the fairly narrow sphere demarcated by 'discipline'.

Finally, there will be some occasions on which we should hesitate to use 'well-disciplined' or 'badly-disciplined' at all; not now because the kind of task or authority is logically inappropriate but more simply because obedience is either non-existent or so negligible that the terms are out of place. The notion of discipline involves some presumption that the group is meant to be, and is minimally trying to be, obedient: this involves some expectation of obedience. A continuing total lack of such obedience would extinguish such expectation; if pupils constantly paid no serious attention to the teacher at all, we should not say that they were badly-disciplined or even that the discipline was appalling – we should say rather that there was no discipline at all.

We ought now to have gained something which is of particular relevance to practical teaching; that is, an idea of discipline as an educational objective in its own right and not just as a facilitator for education. One might perhaps categorize it under moral or political education. It involves the understanding and practice of a particular virtue, confined to particular types of situation which are nevertheless of great practical importance: roughly, situations which are 'tight' enough (I have used the word 'quasi-military') for us to want to speak of 'discipline' as against more general terms such as 'law-abiding'. This has very little to do with notions vaguely canvassed under such headings as 'autonomy', 'self-discipline', and others, and has to be sharply separated from them.

There are reasons why this particular educational objective is important, and why it is currently in dispute. Briefly, it will appear, to liberally minded adults in a civilized, peaceful and pluralistic society, as if the number of tightly-structured, quasi-military situations in which our pupils are likely to find themselves is small, and as if such situations were either not very important or positively objectionable (perhaps as leading to 'conformism' or 'authoritarianism', or whatever). Conversely there are those who are naturally predisposed to such situations, and who will instinctively favour increasing them (one thinks here of demands to reintroduce military service, perhaps of Outward Bound courses, and so on). Leaving prejudice aside, however, we need to note:

1. It is inevitable that children are born and will spend some years in a situation which is tightly structured in the way described. The family is a group of this kind – so is the classroom and the school as a whole. Notions like obedience, duties, allotted tasks and so on, are here inexpellable notions. If a child did not grasp and act upon the principle of discipline, of obedience to established authority, he could hardly survive at all, and a proper grasp of it is an essential enablement for the child to learn other things.

2. Because of this, 'discipline' – although *per se* only one sub-heading of the general area of contractual obligation, acting out of principle, rule-following and so forth – is inevitably a crucially important area. The family and the school necessarily form the arena of the child's first encounter with the whole business of rules and authority. If he does not grasp the relevant points in this arena, it is unlikely (certain developmentalists might say, impossible) that he will do so later when he comes to wider and less structured contexts in which the word 'discipline' is less applicable.

3. Although not many social groups are 'military', a great many are more like a peace-time army than they are like (say) a university or a collection of bohemian artists. We may legitimately speak of 'discipline' in groups of people building bridges, making cars, digging coal, trawling for fish, and a large number of other cases. It is clear enough that, be our or any other society as 'liberal' as it may, we should not survive very long without adequate discipline in such contexts. And these are the contexts in which most of our pupils will in fact operate.

The contrast between discipline, in the sense outlined, and the quite different notion of being 'controlled' or 'trouble-free', is one which teachers (whether they know it or not) face every day. Not infrequently it produces a conflict of aims. Given sufficient charm, bribes, rewards, etc. or just the willingness to overlook offences, it may be possible to keep a class of pupils trouble-free; if we insist on discipline, we may create more trouble rather than less. (Just as, in some industrial situations, it pays the management to 'square' their workers by any means possible, without worrying about contractual obligations or fair play or anything of that kind; or just as, if you wished to survive as a Roman emperor, you gave donatives to the troops, regardless of whether they deserved it.) Many teachers are in a position where they are doing well if they can survive – it seems a bit much to ask them to take on discipline as well. If they let offenders get away with it, who shall blame them? Bribe the bully, let the tiresome child play truant, put the badly behaved out of the room if absolutely necessary, overlook the rule-breaker, turn a blind eye to the lazy and thank God for the end of term.

It is sometimes said that good discipline has no necessary connections with the *power* wielded by teachers; after all, teachers have sometimes had plenty of power (including power to deploy savage forms of corporal punishment, as in the nineteenth-century public schools) but nevertheless discipline was very bad. Hence, we might think, it is not so much power but rather *authority* that matters; that is, the acceptance by the clients that X has the *right* to obedience (not just the strength to enforce it). Indeed if it were just a matter of power, the motivating thought in the client's head would be 'I had better obey, or else I shall get clobbered', and that, as we have seen, is not the thought characteristic of good discipline. The correct thought is 'Because the *authority* says so'. Hence (the story might go) we need not worry about whether teachers have enough powers; we need only worry about whether their authority is sufficient, about whether they are recognized as having the right to give orders and lay down rules.

There is, however, a basic objection to this, which may be put either philosophically or empirically. Empirically, it is a fairly safe bet that if some authority lacks the power to make its orders and rules stick – the power to enforce obedience – it will rapidly cease to be seen as an authority. At most, it will be an authority *de jure* and not *de facto*: the client might say 'Well, I suppose that ideally so-and-so ought (one might put 'ought' in inverted commas here) to be obeyed, after all he is legally in charge; but in fact I shall obey someone else who actually has the power, or just act to suit myself'. With the passage of time the *de jure* authority becomes more and more academic, more and more a matter of some moral judgement abstracted from the real world; perhaps there is some sense in which any descendants of the Czar have the right to rule in Russia, but in fact the authority is now lodged in the Communist Party. Philosophically, and in one way more severely, we might rely on an earlier argument and say that social authorities (not other kinds of 'experts') must by definition be able to issue *rules*, and that unless rules are characteristically backed by enforcement and disadvantaging they are no longer rules: if the authorities do not have the power to make the rules stick, they have become (*pro tanto*) advisers or representatives of ideals rather than authorities. There is, in fact, a (loose) conceptual connection between authority (in this sense) and power.

The argument shows only, though importantly, that power is not a *sufficient* condition for discipline (since *per se* it does not generate the correct motivating thought). Certainly, it is a necessary condition. Even with mature adults, the law would not be the law (but only a set of pious hopes or ideals) unless ultimately backed by some kind of force or power: not because people will only obey the law through fear of punishment – they might have many more high-minded reasons for obedience – but because there must be some back-up to ensure obedience when these high-minded reasons fail. *A fortiori* with children, particularly young children, they may come to recognize and accept the authority of teachers and parents without the constant need for demonstrations of power; but if that power were not there as a background they would not be so accepting of an *authority*.

The Findings

Phase I
We could distinguish (not without difficulty) four basic models or pictures sparked off by introducing 'discipline' into our non-directive interviews. These fell very sharply into two pairs, the members of each pair being much harder to distinguish than the pairs themselves. The models were:

A. *Obedience*. This corresponds more or less to the concept of discipline as explained earlier; roughly, the obedience to legitimate authority as such.

B. *'Respect' and 'good behaviour'*. This picture was painted in terms of a certain mental attitude and behaviour pattern adopted by the young towards their seniors and those in authority. The attitude was far wider than that of obedience (A above): it involved what was constantly referred to as 'respect', together with many items of behaviour connected sometimes with 'respect' and sometimes with a highly generalized moral outlook. Examples are: avoidance of 'bad language', certain styles of dress, and a degree of conformity or even submissiveness. It was often hard to tell whether these items were seen as illustrations of 'obedience' (so that the model is really that in A above); sometimes this seemed to be so, but more often they were seen as representing a preferred ideal entertained by adults, not just as obedience to particular orders or rules.

C. *Fraternity and enthusiasm.* This picture, very far removed from the proper use of 'discipline', was one in which pupils cooperated with adults (not only teachers) in a task either because (a) there was a warm, fraternal feeling between the two parties, and/or (b) the task itself generated enthusiasm. In both cases the pupils were seen as, in a political sense, *equals*. There was to be a collective desire to engage in the task, rather than any orders being given *de haut en bas*. Readers will recognize a very salient, indeed almost orthodox, attitude amongst many modern educationalists.

D. *Self-discipline.* Closely connected with C, but more rarely mentioned, was the idea that discipline (or, as several respondents said, 'any discipline worth the name') had to be internalized: the pupil should control and order himself, as against the kind of background depicted in C.

Clearly A and B go together, as do C and D. Behind each pair there is a generalized style, attitude or regime which the respondents preferred. It is arguable that we should not have even attempted to distinguish A from B, or C from D. But distinctions were possible, since many respondents fell quite unequivocally into only one category; many, for instance, mentioned C without introducing D at all (even after a suggestion to that effect), and vice versa – though A and B were more homogenized. On the whole, however, we should advise the reader not to lay much stress on the figures representing individual categories, and attend rather to those representing the two pairs.

Figures for Discipline (Phase I)
(percentages)

Model	Parents	Pupils	Teachers	Educationalists
A	64	72	44	11
B	24	21	27	29
C	7	1	21	41
D	5	6	8	19

For age:

Model	10–13	14–18	19–25	25–40	40–50	50 and over
A	65	54	31	36	46	78
B	35	31	45	18	32	15
C	0	2	4	15	11	1
D	0	13	20	31	11	6

For sex:

Model	Male	Female
A	34	28
B	31	41
C	17	11
D	18	20

For type of school:

Model	Independent	Grammar	Comprehensive	Primary/Middle
A	71	70	35	20
B	11	14	16	7
C	1	2	34	72
D	17	14	15	1

For social class:

Model	U	Non–U
A	34	46
B	15	25
C	41	23
D	10	6

For educational theory:

Model	Heavily influenced	Not much influenced
A	16	61
B	13	24
C	60	11
D	11	4

For responsibility:

Model	Holding or having held responsible posts	Not holding or having held responsible posts
A	73	27
B	14	30
C	10	31
D	3	12

For tough–minded/tender–minded:

Model	Tough–minded	Tender–minded
A	61	12
B	14	21
C	1	58
D	24	9

For autism:

Model	Serious	Autistic
A	81	8
B	1	13
C	0	41
D	18	38

Phase II

Partly for the sake of tidiness, but chiefly because it happened to work out that way, we were able to split up our interviews and conversations in Phase II under twenty headings. This does not mean that the conversations were split chronologically into twenty parts, but rather that we aimed at getting the respondents to answer twenty questions; according to how the conversation went, we might (and usually did) have to move from one question to another and back again, without much regard for any structure. In all cases, however, we continued the conversation until we were satisfied that we had a pretty firm grasp on how the respondents felt.

The twenty questions are not, of course, straightforward questions with yes-or-no answers. Many of them are large and difficult questions, on which whole books might be written: we wanted simply to determine the main lines of the respondents' thinking. They fell roughly under three headings:

I. *Conceptual clarity.* Here we were concerned only with respondents' logical or conceptual grasp. These questions were (for reasons given earlier) perhaps the most important, but we did not usually ask them first; to do so, we found, tended to inhibit the respondents – as if they were being asked some sort of examination question. They were:

  1. Did the respondent grasp that discipline had to do with obedience? '

  2. (ditto) . . . with obedience to legitimate authority as such (not for any old reason)?

  3. (ditto) . . . the necessity ('value') of discipline in schools?

  4. (ditto) . . . discipline in life generally?

  5. (ditto) . . . the need for rules backed by sanctions?

  6. (ditto) . . . the need for the authority's legitimacy and power for *educational* purposes only?

II. *Empirical fact.* Here we were concerned with views on what was, or would under certain circumstances be, the case. They were:

  7. Was discipline adequately understood in most schools?

  8. Was it adequately enforced?

  9. Was lack of enforcement due to lack of nerve and clarity, or other factors?

  10. Would parents willingly contract to have it adequately enforced?

  11. Would pupils willingly contract to have it adequately enforced?

12. Did pupils prefer existing disorder to more discipline?
13. Given the present state of the law, could discipline be adequately enforced?

III. *Suggestions for improvement.* Here we were concerned with some rather obvious suggestions, which they might or might not endorse. These were:

14. Should sanctions (of whatever kind) be sufficiently strong to ensure obedience?
15 Should teachers be trusted with the power to operate these sanctions?
16. Should there be a right of appeal by pupils against teachers, at least in some cases?
17. Should rules, contracts and sanctions be clearly and fully spelled out in schools?
18. Should the headteacher have more or less ultimate authority in matters of discipline?
19. Should some disciplinary powers be delegated to 'prefects' or other selected pupils?
20. Should discipline and authority be paid more attention to (in contrast with other educational objectives, e.g. academic or vocational knowledge and skill)?

Notes on the questions

I. Most of these have, I hope, been sufficiently clarified earlier. Question 5 required the person to grasp the difference between a rule and an ideal, wish or pious hope (i.e. that rules are backed by sanctions). The only major uncertainty lies in Question 6, which involves the drawing of a distinction between educational (and hence legitimate) authority and extra-educational (and hence illegitimate) authority. I do not deny that this is a hard distinction to draw, but in many cases there is a tolerably clear difference between rules and discipline required by pupils (people as *learners*) in schools, and pupils seen in some other light, e.g. as needing to be turned into good little Fascists or Communists or Christians or respectable middle-class citizens or whatever. The educational criterion, 'Is this necessary for their learning?', is narrower than the infinitely wide, and hence infinitely corruptible, criterion, 'Is this good for them?'. This is discussed elsewhere more fully (Wilson, J. 1979a).

II. Many of the questions in this section, if not all, demand more knowledge or experience than many respondents actually had –

indeed, if we look for answers based on complete information, more than anyone actually has. But we were not looking for this: all had *some* experience of school (most of more than one), and we were looking rather for their interpretation of this experience. In 10, 11 and 12, answers from the relevant categories of respondents were, of course, of more validity in one respect than other answers: yet the correlations are surprising in all categories. Question 13 demanded more knowledge of the law than could be expected of almost all (and in fact the law is pretty unclear in the relevant respects): we aimed here chiefly at finding out whether they thought that discipline could be established without any need to tangle with the law at all (for instance, without excessive physical violence). We did not include directives from headteachers, governors, LEAs, or other such bodies under the head as 'the law'.

III. Many details here had to be spelled out: for instance, in Question 15, how much power individual teachers (probationary teachers, student teachers, etc.) might have; in Question 16, what the 'right of appeal' would actually entail; in Question 18, under what circumstances the headteacher's authority could be challenged; in Question 19, just what prefects could and could not do. Most of these questions, apart from their intrinsic interest, served the purpose of checking to see whether those who, in I and II, appeared to demand more discipline were in fact willing to endorse at any rate some measures required to get it (rather than just believing in it as some sort of ideal); those who answered 'no' to the questions were all asked how, in that case, they would set about ensuring more discipline.

Specified responses
(percentages)

I: grasp of:	A Pupils	B Parents	C Teachers	D Educationalists
1. Discipline as obedience	73	81	56	24
2. Obedience to legitimate authority as such	55	73	31	16
3. Necessity for discipline in schools	91	98	85	53
4. Necessity for discipline in life generally	87	97	93	43

	A Pupils	B Parents	C Teachers	D Educationalists
5. Need for rules backed by sanctions	91	99	71	34
6. Legitimate authority for education only	94	47	53	41

II: belief that:

	A Pupils	B Parents	C Teachers	D Educationalists
7. Discipline not adequately understood in schools	94	99	31	30
8. Discipline not adequately enforced in schools	90	99	65	41
9. Lack of enforcement chiefly due to lack of nerve and clarity	89	98	16	31
10. Parents would contract for enforcement	93	91	43	30
11. Pupils would contract for enforcement	83	73	38	27
12. Pupils did not prefer existing disorder	100	74	63	13
13. Discipline enforceable in existing state of law	91	98	31	30

III: prescription that:

	A Pupils	B Parents	C Teachers	D Educationalists
14. Sanctions be strong enough to ensure obedience	98	99	63	43
15. Teachers be trusted with power to operate these sanctions	81	80	56	37
16. There be right of appeal by pupils against teachers	100	98	90	98
17. Rules and contracts be clearly spelled out	98	82	63	52
18. Headteacher have ultimate authority subject to appeal	73	81	61	34
19. 'Prefects' be used for discipline	71	63	42	21
20. More attention paid to discipline and authority	92	99	78	56

CHAPTER FOUR
Notes and Conclusions

We begin with a simple but (as we shall see later) typical story. An acquaintance of ours teaches 12 – 13-year-old children in an Oxford school. Though the school is not in a particularly favoured area, it is not in a particularly tough one either; and Oxford in general is hardly a blackboard jungle. Teachers in, say, Smethwick, Liverpool, or some districts over which the ILEA might, from its title, be supposed by the ignorant to exercise some educational authority, would regard our acquaintance's position as very desirable. He is not a martinet, but teaches with enthusiasm and clarity; both inside and outside school he shows as much willingness and competence as most teachers, and as much seriousness about education as any.

Two or three private lanes form the exit to the school grounds. At the end of one or another of these, some of his pupils sometimes lie in wait for him. On some occasions they merely taunt him or throw stones; on others they pull him from his bicycle and set about him, if not with the ferocity of A-level thugs, at least achieving an O-level standard of intimidation and minor damage. He now usually waits in the background, asking other members of staff whether there are any children lurking or not; or uses the advantages of speed and surprise to escape down one of the unguarded lanes. This particular activity has been going on for some weeks.

The interest of this story does not lie in the bare facts: they could be paralleled, indeed capped, by far more horrific tales elsewhere. When we mentioned it to a friend from New York, he said, 'That's peanuts. In our school we've more or less given up teaching altogether; we have a very good alarm system, though, and we can bring the cops in with their dogs in thirty seconds flat. Of course, we need to have guards to protect us when we come to school and leave it; in fact we've just requested armed guards – some of those kids are real rough'. The facts are familiar enough. More important are the attitudes and the mechanisms that lie behind the facts.

I give, at the risk of verbosity, the full transcript of the conversation with our acquaintance (A):

Q: That's pretty awful, what are you going to do about it? Or why haven't you done something about it already?

A: Well, there's not much I can do. You see, these particular kids are a rough lot: they come from a pretty bad background. Of course, if the social services were better, and there was a proper community centre . . .

Q: Yes, no doubt something could be done to improve things. But as it is?

A: Perhaps it's my fault for not being interesting or stimulating enough as a teacher. Or perhaps I try to be too firm or authoritarian with them; they won't stand it nowadays, you know.

Q: But you don't make them jump to attention and march about like Nazis, do you?

A: No, but I do try to get them more or less to do what I tell them, you know, to sit down and not shout *all* the time, and not bully the smaller boys, and so on. Perhaps I shouldn't try. Most teachers just attempt to persuade them, and leave it if the persuasion doesn't succeed.

Q: Well, anyway, why not go straight to the headmaster?

A: That's a bit complicated. You don't know our headmaster. I have sent one or two of the rougher kids to him before. He just talks to them – what else can he do?– and perhaps to their parents. That doesn't seem to do much good. I wouldn't want to confess that it's got to this stage: my job might be at stake, and anyway it wouldn't look good on my record, would it? I can more or less keep a sort of control in class, and I just hope it'll die down.

Q: What about punishing them?

A: Well, you can keep them in detention – if you plan it well in advance and send notes to the parents and so on. Rather pointless really, I've tried it sometimes. That's about all you can do. There wouldn't be much chance of suspending them from school altogether: anyway, that would mean making it all public. There's nothing you can do really: there are laws against using any kind of force with them, and there just isn't a disciplinary structure in the school which can actually make it stick if anybody tells them to do something they don't want to do.

Q: That sounds pretty alarming. What about going to the parents?

A: Some of them might cooperate, but it's not surprising that the worst ones won't be able or willing to do much good. It's no good going on at me: I've tried all that, with the help of one or two colleagues. Sometimes it helps a bit, but not much. It's a sort of running battle, and we're the losers.

Q: But can't you get together with the rest of the staff, even if the headmaster won't take a firm line? I bet if you all really meant business, there'd be *some* way of enforcing it.

A: We aren't that collective, I'm afraid. Many would sympathize, but it would mean making demands on the headmaster, or the local authorities or somebody, and it's safest to keep quiet and accept the system as it is. Nobody wants to stick their neck out.

Q: What about your union? Won't they help?

A: The same applies; it would mean making me into a special case. You can imagine how the headmaster would react to *that!* Anyway, so far as I can see, my union hasn't got a particularly firm line on discipline – it's just passed a resolution against corporal punishment, and seems to have all the usual progressive ideas about education. I suppose I sort of have them myself, only they're wearing a bit thin. It's practically impossible to educate people by *any* system if they won't even cooperate. Actually, some of them don't even turn up – and usually I'm thankful for it!

Q: What actually happens in your school if some disciplinary problem is raised? I mean, doesn't the head or the deputy head, or a housemaster or *somebody* have the power and responsibility to fix things?

A: Well, what usually happens is a series of committee meetings in which 'the case is discussed'. By the time any sort of decision is reached, it's usually days too late, and anyway, like I say, nobody can actually *make* the kids do anything. The system keeps going, really, by a sort of mixture of bluff, coaxing and minimal goodwill. It just happens to have broken down a bit dramatically in my case.

By contrast, consider the following letter sent by a housemaster in another school. One boy in particular had been giving a lot of trouble, though he had not got so far as assassinating the teacher; and the housemaster sent copies of the letter to the headmaster, the boy's parents, the boy himself and the local authority:

Dear —,

I thought you would like to know the state of play in regard to N—'s education at this school, which is beginning to border on the non-existent. It is not possible to educate anyone without a certain minimal obedience. We do not, of course, expect obedience throughout, nor do we much mind the occasional demonstration of aggression and violence: boys will be boys. But it is clear that N— is basically and radically unwilling to do what he is told by his classroom and other teachers; and this means that we are doing no more than keep him in school during school hours, exercising (with difficulty) some custodial care but no educational authority.

As his housemaster, I consider that he must first and foremost learn this minimal obedience, and to accept the authority of his teachers. I have naturally discussed his background and personal problems very often, both with him and with others; besides what may be done by way of pastoral care, it is necessary for him to accept this authority if he is to receive much profit from being at school at all. I am very willing, indeed anxious, to bring all available methods to bear on him in this respect, and am confident that I can induce such acceptance, if empowered to do so by those to whom I am, in this job, responsible. The method I have in mind would not involve physical brutality, but would certainly involve complete firmness and entire concentration on the learning of obedience or discipline; obviously we should have to concentrate on this before he could spend much time on other educational objectives. I should require, therefore, at this stage virtually complete control over his school hours, and a *carte blanche* for much of his time after school. If he is to be here, he must – before all else – learn to accept (however grudgingly) the basic rules.

I hope, then, that I can be clearly empowered to perform this (as I see it, educationally essential) task. If not, I feel I must decline *any* responsibility for N— at all.

> Yours etc.,
> X—

The headmaster, who was sane and unafraid, added the following note to the parents and local authorities:

Dear —,

It naturally goes without saying that I entirely endorse what Mr X has said about our pupil N—M—. N— has been fortunate in having so conscientious and capable a housemaster, who has given him far more of his time than could be given to everyone. I confidently expect that, since I am paid to control the education of pupils at this school, his request will be granted: you may consider it my request also.

Yours etc.,

Y—

The local authorities, less sane and more timid, wrote a long screed which included the following:
'. . . whilst we have every sympathy with your problems, we think it right that N—M— should partake of the learning of normal school subjects with other pupils . . .'
together with other chit-chat of a quasi-educational, quasi-political nature. To this the headmaster replied:
'What you ask is impossible. He can be 'with other pupils', though I shall not adopt this course, which would be bad for both him and the others. He cannot 'partake of learning' with them, because he will not learn: and he will not learn, because he will not obey. If you have anything intelligible and helpful to say, I shall be pleased to hear it: otherwise I must regard this correspondence as now closed'.

When everyone outside the school (the boy's parents and the local authorities) and inside it (particularly the boy himself) realized that the headmaster meant business, the problem cleared up in a remarkably short time. After a couple of trials the boy, not being daft, realized that – whatever else might happen – *he would not be allowed to get away with it.* Nobody beat him, or treated him as an outcast, or regarded him as a mental case; he was simply made to obey – and when he did not immediately, he was (as it were) put into suspension until he did, being taken away from whatever he was doing and put into a small and unbreakable room by himself. A contract was presented to him, with the basic rules spelled out, over and above the agreement to obey his teachers in general. Pretty soon he signed. He had no other option.

These stories exemplify, in a rather journalistic way, the two most important features of this sort of situation. There is a great deal to say about disciplinary systems, legal regulations, the function of various teachers and tutors, the help we can get from psychology and sociology, the role of parents and local authorities, pastoral care, and so on. The two most relevant virtues, however, stick out a mile. They are, first, *clear-headedness*, and second, *nerve*. It is (1) *seeing clearly* what is required for education, and (2) having the *confidence to act* on it, which are absolutely necessary conditions for dealing with such matters: these are often also sufficient conditions.

The two virtues are related to each other. It is often *because* teachers and others do not understand what education requires by way of discipline, control and so forth that they do not have the nerve to meet the requirements. More positively, *if* or *in so far as* a person is really clear-headed, in so far as he really has a firm and comprehensive conceptual and intellectual grasp of the matter, then to that extent he has at least the initial confidence which is necessary – that is, confidence in seeing what is required, even if more confidence is needed to produce it. Our impression is that most teachers are stuck at the first stage: for various reasons, many of which are forced upon them, they find it hard even to be intellectually clear about the problems. How much nerve they would have if they had the initial clear-headedness is anyone's guess: in our judgement, more than enough. The real enemy is muddle, not – or not just – cowardice.

Teachers have, in fact, a great deal of power or means of pressure at their disposal – particularly if they combine (even within a single school). Apart from strike action, they can influence how much the child learns, whether he is entered for certain examinations, whether this or that kind of references are given to his first employer or to other educational institutions, and – perhaps most important of all – whether the child is himself subject to bullying, extortion or terror at the hands of other children. It would not be difficult for teachers to demand, and get, the powers needed to do their job properly, by threatening to do only what was required of them by law if they did not. The message to parents and others would be to the effect of, 'If you do not give us the required powers, we predict that your children will be less well educated, less likely to get jobs, less able to pass examinations, and less protected from harm done by other children. Now, do you want us to have the powers or not?' I should be very surprised, particularly in view of our findings, if the majority of parents did not assent.

It is not our purpose, however, to discuss power politics. So far as practical action is concerned – I mean, our chances of actually doing something in education which will be of real use to teachers and pupils – it must be appreciated that we cannot change ourselves or our system unless we understand more exactly what the opposition is that we have to overcome. Without this, things are likely to go on in the same dreary way, or perhaps even to deteriorate: clearly no amount of research (nor, indeed, any amount of sermonizing or politicizing) will help us.

There are, of course, different kinds or levels of opposition. We might talk about the legal or conventional structures which inhibit the practice of discipline, or the less formalized norms which govern people's thinking and behaviour (the 'climates of opinion', 'educational fashions', etc.), or, as we have already done, the intellectual fallacies and logical misperceptions which dominate our minds, or the basic fantasies and psychic states which must generate these misperceptions. A grander or at least more orthodox and respectable looking research project might treat each of these kinds or levels under a separate heading: professional lawyers or administrators might talk about the legal system governing schools and teachers, a sociologist or social psychologist about the less formal norms and climates, a logician about the fallacies, and a clinical psychiatrist about the fantasies. Whilst an extension of our work on these lines is much to be hoped for, there is here some danger of over-specialization. It is likely to be the case that some one or more very *general* ideas or (in Aristotelian terms) 'practical syllogisms' dominate the entire scene and permeate all levels. We need, at least, some non-specialized and jargon-free account of a general kind which will tell us, in simple terms, why we do not do what we can see (in our saner moments) that we ought to do.

These underlying syllogisms or psychic states are, of course, likely to be largely unconscious, and we therefore turned to several consultant psychiatrists for advice and interpretation. We are extremely indebted for their help (though they too must remain anonymous), and found that what they said chimed in tolerably well with our own interpretations – apart that is, from a certain tendency to cast interpretations in the language of some particular psychoanalytic theory. This may, of course, mean that both we and they are mistaken. This in turn raises the question of what counts as proof or verification for such interpretations. I am content here to say simply that (1) they seem to make sense of what is said (in the conversations) and done (in practice), and (2) they were found to be helpful by those subjects with whom we were able to converse long enough on the matter (about 60). Whilst not denying that these two points – even if they could be established satisfactorily here – would not amount to proof, I think the interpretations are at least worth consideration.

To speak very generally, then, and in a sense to offer a conclusion in advance, we might say that the basic problem here is the *toleration of being separate*. Exercising discipline and imposing sanctions involve distancing oneself from the other person in obvious ways. First, one is acting not as an equal or a friend, but as an impersonal authority and in a sense, therefore, not as a person at all, though one still remains a person when exercising this authority. Secondly, one is acting contrary to the desires of the other, i.e. preventing him from doing what he wants, perhaps making him suffer (by sanctions or the temporary withdrawal of affection) in fairly clear-cut ways. The problem is to continue valuing oneself when one has, to put it dramatically, made temporary enemies of other people.

One way of solving this problem, now difficult to adopt for liberals in this and many other societies, is to see oneself as in touch with or sharing in some *external* source or sponsor of values. To take an extreme case, if a man sees himself as the prophet of the Lord, or as ordained by the Party to keep the revolution going, or whatever, he will be able to alienate himself from others because they are, so to speak, not his real spiritual home: his real home is with the Lord or the Party. Victorian parents in this society – at least by repute – kept their nerve in respect of discipline by these means: they felt and believed that they were on the side of the Right, not in the psychically weak sense that they believed in the rationality of what they enforced, but in the much stronger sense that they felt the Right to have some sort of solid existence external to themselves – if not bound up with God, then at least more substantial than the apparently weak notion of 'being reasonable'.

Suppose now, as seems to be the case with many people, that this feeling is denied us. We now feel that we have no solid *locus standi* as authorities at all. We cannot, as it were, be fathers ourselves, because there is no solid father with whom we can identify and be at home. The only alternative, as it seems to us, is that we must all be children: all on the same level, sharing and enjoying things together without the need for rules, regulations, authorities, punishments and the whole apparatus of discipline. For this seems to offer us an alternative home, a tender-minded environment of 'messing in' with our equals, in an atmosphere of 'care, 'concern' and so forth. The fantasy is one of small children playing happily together, enjoying things for their own sake, being 'convivial'. If (we feel) we can really make this work, then we need not be separate: there may be no external powers to join up with, but there will always be our friends, fellow-workers, comrades, chums, mates, etc.

Many contemporary phenomena may be quoted as instances of this basic fantasy. We may mention, heterogeneously and in no sort of order, the vast quantity of left-wing or progressivist writing (Illich and so on) which stems either from Marxist fears of 'alienation' and/or Rousseauesque feelings about the support and friendliness of 'nature': the ethical relativism which has infected even moderately respectable philosophical circles: the extremist phenomena of youth groups (the hippie communes, squats, and so on) which demonstrate the fantasy of infantile sharing in a clear form: the passion for 'integration' and 'breaking down barriers' – both in terms of distinctions between school subjects and in terms of differences between types of pupils ('mixed ability', etc.) – which itself shows the fear of separation or isolation in any form, and the general fashion for 'participation', 'democratic consultation' and the like which has overtaken so many institutions in higher education and elsewhere.

One important feature relevant to all this – whether it be best described as an aspect or a consequence of the fear of being separate – is the *absence of trust*. At the level of rationality, it is entirely plain that we have to trust people with authority and power in order to get certain jobs efficiently done, or done at all. The actual delegation of power, however, depends on the existence of some kind of trust, which in turn may be seen as dependent on being able to tolerate filling some place or position in a hierarchy or structured system. This sort of place-filling is not only tolerable but positively inviting if, though only if, we accept and feel at home with the criteria by which the places are allotted. If we are not at home with them, we feel isolated and separated. To fill the place, and allow other people to fill their places, is thus ultimately dependent on the tolerance of separation. Either we feel reasonably secure in our separateness, and say things like, 'Oh, well, he is the teacher (policeman, expert, etc.) after all', 'He's a reliable chap, let him get on with the job', and so on, or we do not feel secure, and try to drown our isolation by huddling together in committees, 'participating' or trying to get some 'general consensus' by constant chatter.

Plato and a long line of later thinkers believed that it was possible and desirable to impose authority from above, and to make such imposition permanently effective. There are at least some doubts about its desirability. Yet even if it were desirable, the psychic roots of the opposition – if our suggestions are at all near the mark – cast even more doubt on its possibility. One might, indeed, imagine a society (one version could resemble Orwell's *1984*) in which authority was successfully imposed by sufficient psychic control; yet even the permanence of this is questionable, and for nearly all actual societies as they are today the possibility is an academic one. This means that the only way forward, especially for our own and similar societies, must be by the achieving of greater *understanding* of discipline and authority: from there comes the emotional and practical acceptance of them.

There are, I think, reasons why such understanding and acceptance must *begin*, at least, by greater conceptual clarity. It might be supposed, as an alternative, that 'common sense' or 'experience' will eventually do the trick: perhaps things will eventually both be and seem so bad to ordinary people that there will be a 'swing of the pendulum', a 'backlash' in favour of authority. But the trouble with this is that such swings may be no more than the take-over of one fear by another: the dread of chaos, rather than separation, may take its turn to invade the ego and produce certain kinds of arrangements – an obsessive puritanism, or dictators, or whatever. But greater rationality can only emerge if we *learn* from these swings. Characteristically, neither individuals nor societies 'return to common sense' *simply* under the pressure of dramatic events: such pressure is much more likely to drive them further in the direction of the nonsensical and the doctrinaire.

Our main conclusions will, I think, already be clear from preceding remarks. In Phase I, at least, there was in many respondents remarkably little understanding of discipline. Also tolerably clear is the fact that this went hand in hand with, or formed part of, a general failure to understand or practise the whole set of concepts marked by 'authority', 'rules', 'punishment', and so on. This failure has itself to be understood, if only in general terms, before we can be sure that any suggestions we make are on target.

To put things fairly bluntly, and without the benefit of more sophisticated sociological or psychoanalytic theory, it is as if most of us still thought of authority in the way that members of a very primitive society or very young children might think of it – not as a necessary piece of equipment to get certain things done, but in a semi-magical way (rather as one might believe in 'blue blood' or 'the divine right of kings'). Many of our respondents were either 'in favour of authority' in this sense, or 'against it': most were perhaps ambivalent towards it. Specifically in reference to the teacher's authority, there was clearly a feeling that teachers either should or should not be – to put it dramatically – invested with some sort of numinous power calling for 'respect', if not awe: rather like priests, they were seen either as having this power (and therefore they ought not to be jostled, sworn at, or treated as ordinary human beings), or as pretenders, 'no better than we are' (and therefore they ought to be stripped of all power).

However fanciful this may seem, it at least fits the numerous remarks which had no connection with *rational* authority at all – the constant reference to sex, bad language, dress and so forth. I do not say that these features are unimportant if, as may well be the case, they are connected in the *pupils'* minds with the power of teachers; just as, although we know that monarchs excrete, simple-minded people might lose respect for the crown if they actually saw them doing so. Such is the power of fantasy or magic. Rational discipline and authority, of course, depend on understanding the point of *entitlement*, of entrusting certain people with certain delimited powers to do a certain job. This is a matter of rules and adherence to rules, not of being swayed by charisma.

For fairly obvious social reasons, which must presumably include at least the rise in power (together with increased leisure, money and articulateness) of a working class now largely alienated from traditional authorities, and perhaps also the natural decay in acceptance of such authority-sponsoring metaphysics as Christianity, respect for visible holders of authority has declined over the last four or five decades (perhaps for longer): I mean, for actual teachers, policemen, statesmen, parents, priests and so forth. But it has not been replaced by respect for rational authority: that seems to be too sophisticated a concept for the ordinary intelligence to grasp, or rather too impersonal a practice for our feelings to accept wholeheartedly. It is *not* the case that, for instance, respect for the law has increased as respect for judges and policemen has diminished, nor that respect for business contracts has grown as fear of bosses has declined, nor that respect for the impersonal rules required to run schools has become greater as the teacher has come to be held in less awe.

All this may be more or less common ground, but it presents a basic problem which may be roughly stated thus: given people as they are – that is, apparently incapable of firmly grasping and using the notion of rational authority – should we (a) try to *educate* them so that they can obtain such a grasp, or (b) give rational authority up as a bad job, and reinforce some kind of non-rational authority? The former move will, of course, naturally appeal to those of a tender-minded and (roughly) 'liberal' disposition; the latter, to those who are more tough-minded, and are prepared to see 'law and order' flourish at almost any cost. In the wider political field, a broad distinction may be drawn between those who look for salvation in terms of more 'democracy', 'participation', 'autonomy' and so forth on the one hand, and those who feel that some society's only hope may lie in 'a strong man', 'a hard line', or even 'dictatorship'; and it is a regrettable symptom of our own intellectual incompetence that the words 'discipline' and 'authority' have come to be associated – wrongly, as we have seen – almost exclusively with the latter.

The most important thing here is to see the lunacy of taking sides. Returning to our question, we can see (a) that there must be at least *some* people who have a proper grasp of the concepts, some 'educated' class, some set of individuals who will be able to transmit their understanding to others, or, in so far as that proves impossible, able to make the right judgements on their behalf. So the desirability of more education about discipline is clear enough. But we can also see (b) that meanwhile the wheels have to be kept turning: that, even if only in order to be *able to educate* people in discipline, our schools (and indeed our society) must be reasonably trouble-free; that we must have order and obedience in the first place if our 'liberal' aims are to be fulfilled. Moreover, there will also always be some people – very young children, near-idiots, psychopaths and so on – who cannot or will not in fact, however hard we try, grasp the necessary concepts: not everything can, in practice, be achieved by education.

Teachers here are in a peculiar, indeed virtually a unique, position, for they have the dual role of (a) educating, and (b) keeping order. Most other people in positions of authority are concerned only with (b), that is, they have to ensure that certain things get done, that certain rules are obeyed – it is not their job, or not primarily their job, to *teach* anybody anything. In the minds of many teachers, it appears, there is a conflict between (a) and (b). It is as if 'educating' or 'teaching' *meant*, for them, something which was essentially 'non-authoritarian', involving only the children's interest, or their willing participation. Hence the term 'discipline' comes to stand (wrongly) for something rather sophisticated and remote from the idea of obedience to authority in a task-like situation; to stand, perhaps, for what might be meant by 'self-discipline' or even something like 'being genuinely absorbed in some activity', or 'wanting to learn'. (Something of the same role-conflict may perhaps be observed in social workers and others.)

But it is entirely clear that *teachers*, at least, *must* be educated in respect of discipline, for they are the people who have the task of educating the coming generation in that respect. Whatever may be gained by educating people, to understand and practise rational authority can only be gained via teachers. The obvious first step, then, must be in teacher-education. I am not saying here that we should delay other steps perhaps equally obvious (and to be discussed later); by 'first', I mean that it has a clear logical priority, that it is a step which we quite evidently *must* take, whatever else we do. Nor, of course, am I saying that we need not bother to educate *other* people – parents, educational administrators, and so on – in this respect, but that the natural priority lies in teacher education. Once teachers themselves have a proper grasp of discipline, they can join us in considering what else needs to be done.

What would this first step consist of? Initially we might want to say that teacher-education should include more 'philosophy', since that subject is concerned with clarifying concepts. That is a correct view, provided that 'philosophy' is used in the right way: to refer to a study and a context of communication in which the meanings of words are properly understood, no particular partisan 'line' is taken about educational or other issues, and the prejudices and fantasies of those taking part are diminished by an increase in their clarity and common sense. All this has to be stressed, because a good deal of what is called 'philosophy of education', particularly when discipline is concerned, in fact does not do this job; rather, it simply reinforces or sophisticates certain fantasies. This vice is, of course, common to all of us; I am not here trying to pass arrogant comments on the writing of other authors. My point is simply that unless 'philosophy' *does* give us clarity and diminish our fantasies, it is of no use and may even be harmful.

If that is so, the important thing for teacher-education is not best represented by saying that student-teachers should 'do more philosophy': for that, in the eyes at least of many administrators and others who influence teacher-education, might simply mean more man-hours, examinations and books, more professors of the philosophy of education, and more high-minded talk about 'the aims of education', 'the basis of ethics', 'schools and society,' and so forth. Not, again, that one would not cast one's vote in favour of 'doing more philosophy'; the essential point here is that the philosophy should be of the right kind.

It might even be plausible to suggest that student-teachers should do *less* in other areas which might be labelled 'sociology', 'psychology', or 'educational theory'. For the responses make it quite clear that what is taught – or at least what comes across – under these headings often reinforces, where it does not actually create, certain recognizable fantasies; fantasies about, for instance, 'the authoritarian teacher', 'intrinsic motivation' or 'convivial institutions'. Very little 'educational theory', indeed, is free of partisan bias. What teachers chiefly need are a clearer head and a stronger nerve. Most 'educational theory' is demonstrably rubbish.

This does *not* mean that student-teachers should spend less time in *hard thinking* and more time in what some quaintly describe as 'practical' training. There is a fashion, stemming perhaps partly from a disenchantment with the usual content of 'educational theory', for laying more stress on this 'practical' side; but this in itself will not and cannot help the students to retain and enlarge their common sense and conceptual competence. They need many man-hours of argument and conceptual discussion, in which a tough-minded accuracy about the meanings of words may help to defend them against fantasy and prejudice. Without this, they have little chance of remaining level-headed in a world of constantly changing educational fashion and pressure.

There is one respect, however, in which 'practical' training may be useful here. Many people, particularly those without the right sort of experience of responsibility and organization, will defend themselves and their fantasies about discipline in almost any context of discussion or argument. Such people need to be shown, in as 'real' and vivid a way as possible, the kind of disasters which follow on fantasy. Ordinary experience in schools – a term's teaching practice, for instance – is often not much use here: they are thereby made accustomed to a system which is itself largely fantasy-based, and in which the disasters of fantasy are not sufficiently apparent. But put a student in charge of (say) a mountaineering party in which people may fall to their deaths, of a business enterprise in which people may go broke, of a sailing-ship in which people may drown, and the pay-off resulting from lack of discipline becomes much more apparent than it usually is in ordinary schools. Common sense breaks through more easily when the disasters and advantages are easily visible.

It also seems important that student-teachers (and not only they) should be helped to recognize fantasy for what it is in some rather more direct way. Although comparatively little work has been done in this field – at least, not in specific reference to education – most of the major fantasies connected with education are tolerably clear, and could easily be categorized: it would be almost as easy to identify these in student-teachers and others. Most competent teacher-educators, in fact, who take the trouble to know their pupils as people, have a pretty good idea of what sorts of fantasies are at work with what pupils – assuming that is, that the teacher-educators themselves are sufficiently sane to do their job. Much is, no doubt, to be learned from clinical psychiatrists and from whatever reasonable forms of 'group therapy', 'counselling' or 'group dynamics' may commend themselves.

Some of the most striking results, I think, relate to the notion of control (rather than that of discipline, though there are connections). To many respondents, as we had anticipated, 'discipline' more or less *meant* 'control'. Though in fact 'discipline' refers to only one way of maintaining control or social order, we felt it worthwhile to find out something about their views on control.

Hardly anybody thought that pupils ought not in principle to be controlled (few people are quite as mad as that), but there was a considerable difference in their views on the *extent* and *methods* of control. Teachers and administrators were much more diffident than parents and (perhaps surprisingly) pupils about both the extent and the methods. Particularly remarkable is the fact that very many parents, and not a few pupils, felt not only that the school authorities should exercise control over behaviour – a point on which they were more or less in line with the teachers and administrators, though much more tough-minded about it – but also that the authorities should exercise more control over the pupils' *work*, not only in school hours but also outside the school; the enforcement of homework was the clearest issue here.

They were also much more prepared to countenance tough-minded methods of control. Some, perhaps ignorant of legal and other facts of life, regarded teachers as feeble or cowardly for not actually applying these methods. 'If you can't clobber him yourself, just you tell me what he's done and I'll make sure he doesn't do it again' was a common idea, particularly amongst fathers. They had at least a firm grasp of the idea that teachers should be respected and obeyed, even if lacking something of the idea of impersonal obedience to authority. Teachers and administrators, by contrast, felt that control was chiefly a matter of being 'stimulating' or 'interesting' (except with regard to certain groups of extremely difficult pupils), that it was somehow *their fault* if they could not interest the pupils in learning and hence control them. They felt themselves to be, not representatives of impersonal authority, but either possessing or failing to possess the requisite techniques or charisma. This was particularly and perhaps unsurprisingly true of younger teachers, and those who had been influenced by recent educational theory.

An interesting point here is that both parents and pupils (more obviously, perhaps, pupils) often did *not*, in their actual behaviour, live up to their ideas. Everyone is familiar with the parent who is possessive about his (her) own child ('Don't you lay hands on my Johnny'), and disobedient or non-respectful pupils are commonplace. The majority of our subjects in these categories said that they had, in fact, behaved thus on some occasions. We did our best, therefore, in the course of the conversations to make sure that their expressed views were actually sincere, and found not only that they were, but that the subjects recognized the partisan or egocentric feelings that governed them and others on such occasions, and partly for that very reason thought control to be all the more important. 'Well, of course you get carried away when it's *you* (your child), you don't think about the rules; but somebody has to keep order and make sure people stay in line, I'd vote for that straightaway', was the general message.

We hence have the rather remarkable fact that the *consumers* – the parents and pupils – are not only willing but anxious, when properly talked to, to have some adequate method of control and give teachers the necessary powers. The teachers and educationalists themselves seemed, in general, to be much more uncertain about it even though they often quoted what they supposed to be the consumers' views in defence of their own uncertainty ('The parents wouldn't stand for it', 'You can't treat pupils like that nowadays', and so forth). With some hesitance, we might account for this by suggesting that, for the kind of tender-minded and quasi-idealistic liberals of which teachers and (still more) educators are largely representative, the mere idea of actually *holding power* produced serious feelings of guilt. Parents, and perhaps also pupils, lacked this disadvantage. They also had the additional advantage of seeing more clearly what naked power is actually like, and why clear-cut and tough-minded forms of control are absolutely necessary to prevent abuse of it. (Anyone who has brought up a family of normal, lively children finds it much more difficult to sustain an idealistic liberalism *all* the time.)

That the notions of guilt and repressed aggression is not out of place here may be suggested by some of the replies from teachers, which indicate a degree of conflict and compulsion far greater than one might casually suppose. 'If the only way you could, in practice, stop one child bullying and torturing another was to make him frightened of you and your power, would you make him frightened?' 'Oh no, I couldn't do that, you shouldn't make anyone frightened, it's wrong.' 'But if that were the only way – I mean, if you didn't have time to do it by love and influence and the force of example?' 'Well, I just couldn't, I just couldn't live with myself if I did.' 'But doesn't bullying make you very angry?' 'Very, but that's all the more reason to control myself.' 'So you'd just let the bullying go on?' 'Well, I suppose I'd have to: perhaps I could tell the little child to keep out of the big one's way.'

Something of the difference between what is felt by at least some teachers and what is felt by other people in authority emerged fairly clearly in a short study made by two of the team, in conjunction with this particular project, of a school cruise. (Perhaps we should say in advance that in our judgement, for what it is worth, these cruises are admirable institutions for all sorts of reasons. Also this cruise may well have been atypical.) The teachers, who went with the pupils, exercised far less control over them than the ship's officers, not because they had less power or for any other reason, but plainly because the whole *exercise* of authority did not come so naturally to them, and because they lacked confidence in themselves as holders of authority. The officers, who treated the children with much more firmness and even severity, became objects of respect – and, rather strikingly, affection and attachment – much more quickly than the teachers (who, in most cases, were not originally known to the children any more than the officers were). We do not imply any general praise of naval officers at the expense of the teaching profession; but it was clear that they had the immense advantage of working within a clear and properly enforced disciplinary structure. It is significant that their authority was of more value, *even for the purposes of education in this context*, than that which the teachers vaguely attemped to wield.

This may generate the suggestion that, so far from writing teachers off as weak-kneed liberals, most of the problem may be due to the fact that they do not *have* to control the pupils – or at least, only minimally, for the sake of public relations – so that they are not forced into exercising authority by sheer necessity: that they are not *encouraged* to do so effectively by colleagues or other educationalists: and that they are not *enabled* to do so by the existence of a proper disciplinary structure which gives them an adequate backing. If any fault lies with the teachers, it is that they are either not clear-headed enough, or not courageous enough, to demand the control which they clearly ought to have. In this respect, as perhaps in some others, teachers appear as an oppressed and under-privileged class, deferentially accepting what is thought to be (but is not) current public opinion about their proper powers and scope.

Some of the trouble here lies simply in the common inability to imagine 'the system' as anything radically other than it actually is. In many of our conversations we raised the possibility that teachers in state schools might have something of the independence and control enjoyed by, for instance, at least some members of staff in the independent boarding schools (housemasters and others). The very idea seemed to some of them so novel as to be virtually incomprehensible: it was as if we had offered them the vision of a totally new world. The newness was, in general, alarming for most, though attractive for many; they responded to the possibility of power or influence in predictable ways. The majority fell back on reasons why this would, in any case, be impossible except under the peculiar conditions which apply to the independent boarding schools, 'You can only do that if they're boarders', 'Their parents have chosen to send them there, ordinary parents wouldn't stand for it', 'They're all upper-middle-class pupils, it wouldn't work with the rest', and so on. Whether or not any of these reasons actually have force (arguably none have), they were not deployed for their intrinsic merits. As they saw it, 'the system' was what it was, and somehow there must be reasons for it, otherwise the conflict between what is and what might be would seem intolerable.

In all this, it is worth repeating, the teachers are much to be pitied rather than blamed. Not so the educationalists. They do not have to face large classes of undisciplined children every day, without any semblance of power or effective means of control: consequently they are free to exercise their fantasies as researchers, teacher-educators, inspectors of schools, committee members, politicians, or general commentators on education. In imposing these fantasies on those who do the actual work, however, they are much at fault. All of us have our fantasies, but those of us who are in positions of intellectual influence ought to take particular care to keep them to ourselves.

Educationalists and administrators have rarely been in positions requiring *disciplinary* control; that is, as we have seen, control over small groups in task-like situations. The most common case of such experience was some kind of military service: however, the structure and back-up for authority was so strong and clear, in that particular case, that they were perhaps not brought up sharply against disciplinary *problems*, or if they were, the mechanisms for resolving those problems were simple and effective. This is unlike the cases of, say, being the foreman of a recalcitrant gang of workmen, a youth leader, or any similar role where the powers and effectiveness of authority are less obvious. It is, indeed, rather hard to find even moderately close analogies with the teacher's role because the need for discipline is unusually great and its enforceability unusually small. Senior army officers who have successfully controlled large forces in desert warfare have been known to be reduced to rubble when trying to control the Lower Fifth. From this point of view, one very important obstacle to improvement is simply that the present state of affairs is regarded as acceptable. Children are often no longer expected to obey, attend, and remain reasonably silent: perhaps 'reasonably' is construed well below the level of what reason in fact demands. 'An acceptable noise level', for instance, is often one in which the teacher has to make a special effort to be heard. Any teacher who actually wants to *teach*, of course, will naturally often want virtually *no* noise and virtually *total* attention; that will be the proper norm, even if it is sometimes or even often broken and, when it is broken, something has gone wrong. But this is no longer even widely regarded as a norm. On the contrary, it is regarded, in many schools, as some sort of airy-fairy ideal, impossible of fulfilment by any means at all. Yet other schools show clearly that it can be easily done.

Another obstacle is the peculiar deference and insecurity which seem to run widely through the public system of education. In most independent schools – certainly in those of any standing (and this is partly why they have achieved such standing) – the relationship between the head and his official superiors (the governing body) is far less fraught than in most state schools. Teachers in the public sector are far more worried about their jobs, their public image, and their relationships with the local authority and with parents than are their independent counterparts. Many reasons contribute to this, but one fairly obvious to anyone who has had adequate experience of both sectors is (roughly) that most teachers in the state system feel themselves to be more vulnerable, less powerful, less confident and less connected to that upper-middle-class and/or upper-class world, amongst the chief characteristics of which is supposed, at least, to be a certain style of self-confidence (often criticized, not always unjustly, as arrogance). They do not feel themselves to be professionals of the same standing as (for instance) the barrister or the doctor. Nor, on the other hand, can or do they identify themselves at all whole-heartedly with working-class sources of power. Many teachers' attitude to the teachers' unions is ambivalent or uncertain.

This deference prevents them from even envisaging, let alone operating, the kind of 'staging' or stage-setting necessary for the deployment of autonomous power (and very obvious in traditional independent schools, where it may require considerable nerve for parents even to question the school's power). Partly owing to fantasies of 'integration', few state schools are so constructed as to reinforce the hierarchical potency of headteachers, or to demonstrate to the outside world that the school is a world of its own with its own values, powers and authority.

Another reason, obviously connected with the above, is that not many people of really high intellectual ability go into education; so that most people in the business are not equipped with at least one possible defence against fantasy and nonsense. It is perhaps characteristic of highly intelligent people that they dislike being told what to do by people plainly more stupid than themselves; either they find themselves an independent niche within the system or they simply escape from it and do something else. It may well be this, rather than any characteristics associated with social class, which chiefly accounts for the deference and lack of secure contra-suggestibility which we have spoken of. A really competent, able, and confident person would just not put up with the position in which many teachers are now placed.

Unfortunately this is true in education generally, not only of teachers. One would not expect, nor perhaps want, most teachers to be of the very highest intellectual quality – the job is largely a practical one, and the required qualities are somewhat different. But such an allowance can only be safely made if these practical workers are supported and guided by people who (or some of whom) *are* of top quality. This is, very obviously, not the case. The most able academics tend *not* to go in for 'educational theory' or for the philosophy, psychology, sociology, etc. of education: it may even be true, though the point is somewhat less obvious, that the most able administrators tend not to go in for educational administration. The whole business has the air, not only of something lacking in glamour or smartness, but of something intellectually second-rate.

There is a vicious circle here, of course. Whilst it looks second-rate, first-class people will tend not to go in for it, and *vice versa*. It is conventional to regard the proper way of breaking this circle as a matter of more money, smaller classes to teach, and so on. Much more plausibly, in our view, it is a matter of giving teachers (and others concerned with education) more *power* or *scope*. There are plenty of first-rate people who are deeply concerned with education, and would be more than willing to make a career in it if only they had sufficient control over their own jobs – as much control as, say, the average parson, or university lecturer, or lawyer. Teaching positions in the independent schools approximate more closely to this ideal; but in most state schools we rely on the services of an oppressed and under-privileged body of people, working under rules and conditions not of their own making, and surrounded by external forces which are often more hostile than supportive.

With many respondents we discussed, albeit rather vaguely, widespread forms of juvenile or semi-juvenile delinquency which would include, for instance, theft, arson, minor forms of violence, damage to property, 'mugging', terrorism and bullying, but excluding the (comparatively) rare offences of murder, rape, or extreme forms of assault. We do not suggest that these latter require a type of treatment which is, at all points, logically different from that required by the former. But we confined ourselves to the former chiefly because one or other of such forms of misbehaviour was within the experience of our respondents.

Undoubtedly the most striking fact here was that the vast majority of our respondents seemed to echo or represent neither what might be thought of (at least if one judges by what appears in the national press) as current *opinion* on these matters, nor what seems to be our society's current *practice* in dealing with them. Current opinion, or those parts of it which publicity is most apt to highlight, includes at least two types of reactions. These are: first, a generalized view of such behaviour as a 'social product' (arising from 'bad homes', 'insufficient space for games playing', 'healthy aggression', or whatever), to be dealt with by some kind of sociological method rather than by the normal application of rules and punishments; second, a sharply retributive reaction ('birch them', 'put them in the stocks', 'send more of them to prison', etc.). Current practice, it seems, is incapable of solving the problems by any method; fines are increased, trouble avoided by banning attendance at football matches, and vast sums of money are spent on prevention and protection ('vandal-proofing' whatever has to be protected), but nothing very effective is done.

Most of our respondents took a different (and, as it seems to us, a saner) view of the matter. They were clear that (a) clear rules and punishments had to be laid down, and properly publicized, for all such offences, (b) the punishments had to be effective as deterrents – that is, sufficiently unpleasant to prevent the misdoers from engaging in such behaviour, (c) restitutive justice should be enforced by making the offenders pay back, in terms of time and effort, for the damage or unpleasantness they had inflicted. Perhaps even more importantly, they mostly believed (d) that some *person* or group of people had to be entrusted with sufficient on-the-spot power to ensure that this apparatus was actually effective. It was widely believed that, if the police, the family, the probation officers and (ultimately) the magistrates were as ineffective as they seemed to be, then for those under school age at least the authority should reside in the school; that is, in the headteacher and whatever other teachers had responsibility for the particular offender.

In some (if few) schools, of course, this is *de facto* the case. If a pupil is detected in, say, the offence of causing damage to property, then – whether or not he comes up before the courts – the headmaster or housemaster will in fact ensure (a) that the pupil has clearly understood beforehand that such behaviour counts as an offence, (b) that he is sharply deterred from doing it again, (c) that he makes good the damage. In other words, condition (d) is satisfied: the school does take on responsibility, and has the power to enforce it, for such occurrences. This responsibility and power are by no means entirely confined to the independent boarding schools. There appears to be no reason, other than the traditional impotence of many schools in our society, why all schools should not do this job. As the replies show, there is little doubt that most parents would wish it. Doubts about it are found mostly, and predictably, amongst educational theorists and administrators.

Here again an external observer, looking at current practice, might suppose that there was general acceptance of some view to the effect that it should be *nobody's* job to ensure that (for example) pupils behaved properly on school coaches, did not vandalize telephone kiosks after school hours, and so forth: as if, knowing that the police could not be everywhere, we vaguely hoped that 'parents' or 'the home' would improve the situation, but did not feel strongly enough about it to empower any authority actually to deal with it. Even when railway carriages are almost totally destroyed, or bus drivers refuse to transport hooligans, we seem to think – or so, at least, is the appearance – that nothing much can be done. That is, indeed, the practice. The notion that parents, teachers, pupils and (I dare say) the public at large do not *want* to empower an authority to deal with it is, according to our findings at least, demonstrably false. They do want to; and in default, at least, of any other kind of 'local disciplinarian' (so to speak) they are anxious for teachers to take on the job.

In our view, what is most alarming is not the actual 'misbehaviour' of pupils in or out of school, the vandalism prevalent in many neighbourhoods, the hooliganism at football matches and so forth. These and similar phenomena are, it seems to us, entirely predictable in the absence of clear and adequate control. *Of course* pupils without discipline will behave in this way: *of course* teenagers, full of energy and excitement, will start fights and smash things up. It is ridiculous to say that they are in no sense 'to blame', being merely 'the products of society'. Yet it is almost equally absurd to say that they are in every sense 'to blame', since that implies some awareness on their part of clear and adequate rules which they deliberately break: though often there *are* no clear and adequate rules. It is rather that the very concepts of blame, responsibility, rule-breaking and so on have, in many areas of behaviour, simply not been introduced into their lives. What precisely (for instance) are they allowed to do on football terraces, and what are they not allowed to do? How are these approved and disapproved items of behaviour publicized, if at all, and does anyone make it *clear* to them? What sanctions are made clear to them, attached to what items? What measures are taken to identify rule-breakers – are the cameras on them, are there people in authority taking notes and names? Since the answers to all these questions are either negative, or at best unclear, it is not surprising that they have no more than a vague idea of 'what they can get away with'.

It is important to appreciate that the desired moves may be made without getting into complicated arguments about 'values' or 'ideology'. The minimal rules required (a) for serious learning to go on in schools, and (b) for pupils in schools to be tolerably happy, or at least immune from non-controversial dangers, are pretty obvious and hardly in dispute. We *know* that pupils should turn up on time, pay attention to the teacher, do their homework, not bully each other, not vandalize property and so forth. These are not items in a particular 'ideology' but necessary conditions for any serious institution of learning. Others, no doubt, are more disputable; for instance, the merits and demerits of school uniforms, organized games, the use of 'bad language', long hair and many other things may be argued about. But these arguments can wait until we have established the necessary minimum.

Our advice would be that those parties to the business of education – whether parents, teachers, pupils or educationalists – who do in fact feel that something should be done should *first* canvass opinion in the case of their particular school. Is it, in fact, true that the school's parents are contented with the present position? Would they (as our own survey suggests that they might) actually prefer something different? It would then be clear on the basis of such an enquiry – not too difficult to carry out, in the case of a single school – just what the demand or consensus is. If, as is likely, some clear idea is gained of what sort of changes would be necessary, there is then every reason in the world to press for such changes by whatever methods seem appropriate.

We also discussed whether things were worse now than they used to be. I have stated this question as vaguely as possible, precisely in order to remind the reader that there will be various answers, depending on *what* things are supposed now to be worse or better and in what *respects*, compared with *when* in the past time. A complete survey of the possible and relevant options is impossible here, but so far as discipline goes, one or two points may be worth making.

First, we have no doubt that the *concept* of discipline in educational contexts, compared with the situation in the UK of, say, thirty years ago, has in fact sunk further below the surface. Indeed it has in some degree passed out of the immediately conscious grasp of many people: that is, it is disappearing or has to some extent disappeared. Evidence for this cannot, of course, be anything like conclusive from our particular sample. Nevertheless, it is certainly highly suggestive that (a) older respondents were conceptually clearer than younger ones, (b) those less directly concerned with education were clearer than those more directly concerned, and, (c) the concept still flourished in some (perhaps nearly all) non-educational contexts (e.g. in questions about ships, the army, and other task-like situations) in the minds of those who had dispensed with it in educational contexts.

Secondly, however, the *practice* of discipline does not lend itself to any reliable generalizations. Certainly it is plausible to say (on grounds not connected with our own research) that children in schools of thirty years ago were more rigidly *controlled*: it may even be likely that they were more *obedient*, that is, more obedient to authority. Being well-disciplined involves, as we have seen, obeying authorities *qua* authorities and not *qua* anything else, and it seems extremely doubtful whether pupils in past ages grasped this idea any more firmly than pupils nowadays; perhaps, indeed, they grasped it less firmly. It is entirely possible that their obedience was due to other factors (most obviously, fear of punishment or some kind of respect for 'charismatic' authority), and that nothing very much has changed except a diminution of that fear, with a corresponding lack of control. That would, indeed, be our guess, a guess to some extent supported by remarks made by older respondents about their own reasons for obedience when they were pupils. Clearly no reliable judgements can be made here, nor (since we cannot now with any certainty enter the minds of pupils of thirty years ago) is it easy to see how any such judgements ever could be made.

Thirdly, though (as has been suggested) control may now be much worse, it is not entirely clear that either the concept or the practice of restitutive justice are in any worse a state. True, the concept and practice are both now at a low ebb. In the past, though retributive justice (with its usual connotations of painful punishment rather than recompense) no doubt flourished more, so that in *this* sense there would be both a stronger theory and practice of 'paying back', there is no very obvious evidence that retribution *qua* straightforward recompense was more favoured than it is now.

This general picture may be true of much contemporary behaviour in our society over a wider spectrum. The diminution of control and obedience to authority (whether or not *qua* authority, and whether or not for the right reasons) is a different matter from the rejection of rational and rationally desirable ends and procedures. One might suspect, indeed, that the grasp which people have of these latter – the degree, so to speak, to which their thought and action are governed by reason – may remain, in a broad way, comparatively constant. Maybe one fantasy simply replaces another, or becomes uppermost at a particular time. What many of us are accustomed to regard as 'security', 'law and order', etc. may be founded on nothing more than a coincidence of (bad) reasons with ends or states of affairs that happen to be desirable.

This does not mean, of course, that control is unimportant. We are concerned (indeed as educators we are particularly or perhaps uniquely concerned) with the advancement of understanding, with people doing things for the right reasons. We are also concerned simply that the right or necessary things should *get done*, that trouble should be avoided, contracts kept, crime prevented and so forth. These states of affairs are good in their own right, and remain of paramount importance even if the reasons for which men act in respect of them are demonstrably absurd. The mere rejection of particular versions or images of non-rational authority, so far from giving any comfort to those of broadly liberal persuasion, should more properly alarm them. If such rejection does not at once give place to the acceptance of a rational authority, and if the rejection also involves the disappearance of control, we simply find ourselves fighting hot or cold wars – a grave situation in which (if we survive at all) the nature of things inevitably imposes a harsher and more tyrannical authority even than the one we originally rejected.

We discussed also the question of why those teachers who understood discipline did not enforce it. There are various answers to this, but we may start with one possibility which is certainly *not* the, or even an, answer. Their failure to enforce it was *not* the result of carelessness, or lack of feeling, or any weakness of will. On the contrary, nearly all the teachers we spoke to were extremely upset, and often very bitter, about the absence of enforcement. They certainly *cared* enough about it. As we have seen, the correlation between those subjects who understood the concept and those who saw its necessity and value was very high – almost all those who realized what discipline was also realized its importance. Why then did they not enforce it?

We have here to distinguish between headteachers (together with those who held offices which had quasi-political or 'public-relations' aspects – some deputy heads, for instance) and ordinary class-teachers. The former group saw their jobs in essentially political or public-relations terms. Their chief aim was, not so much that discipline should be enforced, justice done, and authority clearly perceived, but rather that their school – considered as a political entity, so to speak – should (a) not fall foul of any powerful external body (in particular parents and local authorities, but also the press), and if possible (b) get or retain a good reputation. Their chief anxiety, conversely, was that the *appearance* of something bad (violence, nasty remarks in the press, parental disapproval, etc.) might upset the precarious stability of their position.

In saying this, I do not suggest that all these headteachers were weak-kneed or had an eye to the main political chance. It was clear from many conversations that many of them would ('under ideal conditions,' as was commonly said) have run properly disciplined and well-organized schools. The point was rather that they simply did not have the power: and with the absence of power, there rapidly ensued an absence of nerve to do things which might have been within even their slender powers. They felt, with justice, that under modern conditions, a headteacher simply could not *survive* – at least psychologically, even if he retained his job – if there was more than a minimal amount of 'trouble': it was as if they felt themselves to be sitting on a volcano, trying to keep the lid on. Hence, as is virtually inevitable for those in political positions, most of their energies were devoted to avoiding such 'trouble': i.e. to keeping things going by any available methods.

Much the same is true of the class-teachers, except that they were frightened of their position and repute vis-à-vis the head. They could not, in general, rely upon the head to back them up with sufficient firmness in cases of indiscipline, and they themselves preferred to skate over such cases rather than bring them to the head's attention. They were themselves aware that the head himself lacked sufficient powers to do very much about it, and that he relied on the usual mixture of coaxing, persuading, cajoling, bribing, or simply overlooking pupils who caused trouble, whilst expecting his teachers to do the same. 'I don't want to be a trouble-maker' was, in one form or another, a common thought, or, 'After all, what can we do when it comes to the crunch?'

Although some teachers stood out firmly in favour of some particular kind of sanction (corporal punishment, for instance), we were much surprised at how clear-headed the vast majority were on this point. They appreciated that – the other things being more or less equal – the *type* of sanctions mattered much less than their *efficacy*. 'The only point is, they must learn who's master' was a common idea; equally 'Whatever we do, we've got to make it stick'.

Most realized (what must surely be correct) that *if* it was both true, and seen by the pupils to be true, that the school authorities – whether in the person of the headteacher or individual teachers – *did* have the power to make their orders stick, then cases of indiscipline would greatly diminish. It was, as they saw, establishing this point of principle, i.e. 'who's master', that counted for practically everything. This is little to do with what sanctions are actually employed, or how often, but a great deal to do with the nerve and confidence of those deploying them. Various suggestions were made: that the school should simply stop educating the pupil until he had learned to obey and accepted authority; that some rapid shock-treatment (corporal punishment or something of that kind) be administered until it worked; that persistent offenders should be publicly declared unemployable, or that they should be removed from the school altogether, that they should be kept in detention indefinitely, and so forth. But most subjects held less strong views about the type of sanctions than about their effectiveness in showing 'who's master': an encouraging sign.

Finally, the question may be raised, not now of whether this movement towards the establishing of rational authority and contractual clarity *ought* to be made – that seems to us beyond dispute – but of whether it is in fact *likely* to be made. Here we entertain grave doubts. In some parts of the world, where disciplinary conditions are extremely bad, there have nevertheless been few attempts to reinstate rational authority: continued chaos seems to be preferred, and dissatisfied individuals simply move out (if they can) of the chaotic context. The alternative to reinstating rational authority is a well-known phenomenon; things eventually get so bad all round (not only in schools) that some powerful authority, of a charismatic and non-rational kind, emerges with enough support to take over. Unable to grasp (let alone realize in practice) the notion of rational authority, people then cling *faute de mieux* to the representatives of some specific ideology – usually of a puritanical kind – who will at least 'maintain law and order'. This in turn is doomed to perish, since (because it is non-rational) it carries with it particular values which will, sooner or later, come under attack. And so the wheels turn.

The kind of non-rational authority liable to take over is familiar to us. It is based on a confused but potent picture of the 'good' pupil, 'good' being construed not at all or not only in terms of rational criteria but in terms of a particular life-style. In this vein, the 'good' pupil is perhaps clean and tidy, does not use 'bad language', does not criticize his elders, wears his hair short, is in uniform, does not express his sexual or aggressive feelings in any way alarming to adults, and so forth. Still less rational pictures might include some idea of racial or social class purity, an element of male dominance, strict censorship of 'corrupting' literature and the visual arts, and so forth. That is the kind of price we may pay, if we cannot develop enough clarity and sophistication to make authority work in the right way.

We are not optimistic about the future, if only because of certain obvious truths. The ego and the forces maintaining rationality are, even in the most sophisticated of us, fragile when compared to those of the irrational and the unconscious mind, sparked off and sustained as they are by the pushes and pulls of 'society' and ideology. The virtues of common sense, often supposed peculiarly British, may not be strong enough to survive; already there are signs of a general loss of confidence in public institutions of all kinds, and too many people may simply choose to opt out. (Already there are schools where conditions are such that sensible and well-educated parents say to their children something like, 'Look, you have to sit through this chaos, it's the law: but when you come out at four o'clock perhaps we can teach you something worth learning. Meanwhile just try to survive'. Others, of course, try to rake up the money to send their children to schools where more rational standards prevail.)

On the other hand, there are some grounds for optimism. The clarity and rationality required do not, at least for the respondents in our own survey, lie too far below the surface. In the case of parents at least, whose jobs are not at stake and who are not too deeply enmeshed in a semi-lunatic system to give up all hope of bringing about change, many respondents seemed willing to take the action required. Perhaps there is still time for us to come to our senses. It would, of course, be extremely helpful if educational theorists, politicians, researchers, and administrators were to assist this process, and encourage the thinking of parents and teachers along the lines of reason: that may itself be too much to hope for. Educational research, theory, and administration are largely self-sustaining industries, and have long since severed many of their links with truth and rationality. It may even be fairer to say, they have evolved their own autistic ideas of truth and rationality, disconnected both from any serious consideration of what education logically implies and from the actual desires of the consumers. That sounds harsh, and of course there are exceptions. But it would be rash to hope for much from this quarter in the immediate future. We must rely on reviving and sophisticating however much common sense and sanity still remains amongst the general public. It will be the parents and teachers themselves, together with the pupils for whose benefit the whole enterprise is undertaken, who are most likely to change things for the better.

Part Three

CHAPTER FIVE
Understanding Moral Educati

I have written a great deal (perhaps too much) on this topic, which may serve as some excuse for writing somewhat briefly and crisply here.

The Concepts

Understanding the *basis* of ME is by far the most important requirement, because without it nothing serious can be done, however much money and effort are deployed. ME requires (a) a *non-partisan* approach, that is, an approach derived from pure reason and not from the tenets of any particular creed, culture, ideology or set of social values. As with any other subject or department of life, we have to grasp what counts as 'a good performer in the moral sphere', and list the attributes of such a performer; this has nothing much to do with 'society' or 'a general consensus', but with coming to understand what we would mean by 'being reasonable' or 'being educated' in this area. We have to list these attributes, and show that reason requires each of them; otherwise we are not educating, but merely selling some kind of party line. However, education requires also (b) a *methodology*; that is, although we do not sell the pupils our own right answers just because they are our own, we do initiate them into *how to get* right answers and how to act on them effectively. Again as with any other educational subject, we show pupils what sort of reasons are appropriate, what kinds of procedures and qualities they need to do the subject properly. Without this, we should not be educating them at all. There would be no principles of reason to educate them *in*, and we should merely be giving them scope to 'discuss' or be 'stimulating concern' about moral matters without any suggestion that there were such things as right and wrong answers, wise or unwise decisions, relevant or irrelevant considerations, sane or insane views. (Many current projects do not do much more than this.)

It is a pity that the word 'moral' attracts more interest than the word 'education'. Various societies are liable to various kinds of fear or obsession when the word crops up. One may be frightened of Communism, atheism, clericalism, imperialism, etc.; frightened that educators are going to invade the pupil's private soul, or frightened that the pupil is going to be left in a vacuum without a 'faith to live by', or frightened that moral education will be used for the purposes of some particular culture, or creed, or political cause. The only way out of these fears – and of their corresponding fanaticisms – is to remember that education should have no truck with any of them. 'Moral' must, for educational purposes, be the title of a form of thought or department of life – contrasted with 'non-moral', rather than 'immoral'. It must be taken as parallel with 'scientific', 'historical', 'mathematical', and so on. Just what ground it should cover is disputable and perhaps ultimately a matter of wise decision. There are good reasons for following those philosophers who connect morality with a man's *overriding* principles and behaviour (Hare, R.M. 1963), though others argue that to count as moral such principles and behaviour must be backed by certain kinds of reasons or relate to certain kinds of goods, roughly, connected with other people's interests. In either case, however, the qualities which the educator will hope to instil into his pupils will be much the same (see below).

There are two basic fantasies: they correspond to the requirements above. There is: (a) the fantasy that ME can only proceed by taking as its basis a set of substantive and particular moral values (derived from 'society', or from Christianity, or what Marx says, or some other ideological platform); (b) the fantasy that there are no such things as right answers to morality, that one judgement is as good as another, that 'everything is relative'. In most democratic and liberal societies at the present time the latter fantasy is more common: for fear of any authority or set of standards, we do not even attend to the authority of reason and the standards imposed by, or inherent in, the subject itself. Yet anyone who seriously faces the question 'What ought I to do?' at once commits himself, logically, to a whole set of procedures which are necessary for answering the question properly; that is, to understanding the force of the word 'ought', to an awareness of what a person is and what people's interests, and wants, consist of, and to a knowledge of the relevant facts. This leads on to

the qualities of determination, alertness and so forth which will alone enable him to act on whatever answer he comes up with. These and other attributes are needed by any serious student or moral agent. That is why they can stand as the (non-controversial) aims of ME.

It is worth noting that these points apply to other educational titles that may be preferred to ME, or that overlap with it; for instance, 'social education', 'values education', 'political education', or titles of a still vaguer kind – 'learning to live', 'learning to grow up', 'education in personal relationships', and so forth. I mention this because it seems remarkably difficult for people to grasp the two basic points, (a) and (b) in the previous paragraph, under any heading whatsoever. To take a topical example: in the UK, for one reason or another, the title of 'political education' has recently become more prominent than usual. If one asks what this is supposed to consist of, the answer given in some circles is roughly, 'Pupils ought to know how their political system works (the details of government, the party system, etc.); of course they ought not to be indoctrinated with the views of any one party, but they ought to learn how to play a full part in a democratic system'. That sort of line (recently taken by inspectors of schools in the UK, and much popularized elsewhere) is demonstrably feeble-minded. (1) It may be *bad* to have a 'democratic system' (whatever that may mean) – Plato thought so, and pupils should at least realize that the matter is controversial; for simply to assume that democracy is good because it is (supposedly) in force in some societies is, in fact, a kind of oblique indoctrination; (2) perhaps the 'political system' as we have it is in a high degree irrational, so that a sensible pupil might see its details as intrinsically boring; (3) no indication is given of how pupils can be encouraged to make up their minds *rationally* on political issues, yet that, and that alone, would justify any programme seriously aimed at educating pupils *in* (not just *about*) politics.

So with other titles. We may conduct 'religious education' on some assumption as that religion is a good thing or that there is a purpose to the universe. 'Education in personal relationships' may be based on the assumption, for instance, that people ought to get married or be gentle in their love-making. 'Social education' may rely on the assumption that our particular society, or western society, or some 'consensus' drawn from most societies incorporates the right values; but that gives no rational grounds for the pupils' assent (or, indeed, for our own beliefs). Sooner or later some pupils at least are going to challenge these assumptions. Indeed this happens already. If education is possible in any or all of these (overlapping) areas, it can only be so if we confront the task of working out what can reasonably count as a good (competent, perceptive, sane, etc.) decision-maker and agent in these spheres – if we have some clear idea of what reasons are relevant to them, and what personal qualities necessary. Without that, without any kind of methodology, all we can do is to swap prejudices or stick to the discussion of non-controversial facts: just as, if we did not know how to educate pupils *in* science, all we could do would be to tell them *about* science (about the history of science, its importance in the modern world, and so on), and let them generate their own scientific beliefs unchecked by any rational methodology.

Of the various fantasies sparked off by the words 'moral' and 'morality', perhaps both the commonest and the most obstructive is the idea that these words stand for some *one quality* (rather like being red-blooded), a quality which may in some mysterious way be 'transmitted' or 'infused' or 'caught' or 'inculcated': the agents for this process being 'society', 'the concerned teacher', 'the good example of parents', or whatever. 'Goodness', or 'virtue', or 'morality' somehow spreads by infection or transfusion (like a blood transfusion). It is this fantasy, I think, in one form or another, which causes hostility or indifference to the demonstrably correct idea of putting some aspects of moral education into the curriculum. To 'put morality into the curriculum' sounds a bit like putting God into the curriculum (or Virtue, or The Good, or Love, or something of that kind).

One aspect of this fantasy is the 'But-X-comes-into-everything' idea; it is noteworthy that we do not want to run this idea as an argument against putting X into the curriculum in the cases of (say) science, or mathematics, or English, but feel tempted to run it in other cases ('morality', 'personal relationships', etc.). Of course some people just react against any kind of specialized study at all: I actually heard one teacher say, 'What! Learn mathematics as a separate subject! Ridiculous! Mathematics is all around you', he added, gesturing vaguely. If one is obsessed by the need to 'break down subject barriers' to the point of no return, there is not much that argument can do. But in general people, or educated people, do recognize that there just are different kinds of questions, issues, problems, 'forms of thought', or whatever, even though connections may be made between them. The argument that morality 'comes into everything' will not do, partly because it is not true (plenty of situations do not involve moral choices), and partly because, even if it were, that would not be a reason against giving special curricular consideration to (if one wants to insist on such a description) the 'moral aspect' of 'everything'.

Another aspect is the notion that morality has little to do with *thinking* or *learning* at all: that it is wholly concerned with 'feeling' or overt 'behaviour', and therefore in a strict sense unteachable, and that hence all we can do (or need to do) is just to 'motivate' people in various ways (example, or inspiration, or cold baths and rugger, or tea and sympathy, or whatever). This could only be maintained by somebody who believed that educators were only interested in overt, photographable, 'brute' behaviour, for which the kind of reasons or motives or intentions did not matter. What such a person would want would be not morally educated pupils, but trouble-free ones: we leave him in the hands of Skinner and other operant conditioners, but do not pay him as a teacher or educator. As soon as reasons, purposes, motives and so on are allowed to walk on stage, we at once have to consider what *sorts* of reasons we are going to encourage pupils to use. Now morality can be clearly seen as partly, at least, a matter of thinking, learning, grasping concepts, noting what is relevant and irrelevant, and using what Aristotle called the right 'practical syllogisms': not, certainly, a matter just of a blood transfusion, nor even of some process of 'development' or 'maturation'.

This goes against quite a lot of grain, for reasons I am not clear about. A modified version of the idea above is that 'We all *know* well enough what is right, the problem is to *do* it'. This does not totally abolish the notion of reasoning but relegates it to a minor role. The idea is that we all know that (say) we ought to act out of love for our neighbour, so that there is no point teaching this to children; rather we should get on with the 'motivation', or inspiration, or whatever. One difficulty with this idea is that different people or societies that claim to 'know' make this claim on very different grounds, which not infrequently produce very different types of behaviour. Consider, for example, the 'knowledge', or the sort of certainty, claimed by Christians, Nazis, Communists, members of the IRA and so on. There is indeed such a thing as moral knowledge, but most of us, much of the time, either do not possess it or do not use it as a basis for action. We have a strong resistance to the programme of (i) working out the answers for ourselves in the light of reason, and (ii) prescribing these answers for ourselves to act upon. We find this threatening, and too much like hard work. It is easier to act out our fantasies.

Of course education in morality has different objectives (or, 'being educated in morality' means something different) from those of other departments, just as these other departments differ from each other. But if we keep the parallel with those subjects that have been effectively established in educational practice, we can see the irrelevance of many issues that constantly come into our awareness. Among the most common are:

1. *Society.* What any society may or may not approve or practise or uphold has nothing to do with educational aims. 'Being educated in morality' (science, history, and so on) means the same at all times and in all places; though, of course, in some places it may meet with more opposition in practice than elsewhere. In particular, we cannot derive our aims in moral education from 'society' any more than we can intelligibly derive the meaning of being educated in science from practices of a society of astrologers and witch-doctors. Educating pupils means, roughly, initiating them into those principles and practices of reason that are relevant to particular subjects or departments. These principles and practices are, as it were, transcendental. Mathematics is mathematics, whatever any society may do about it. So too with morality. We do not need, and should not seek, a general consensus; we need only clarity about what reason and logic tell us is necessary for the educated person.

2. *Imposing values.* If someone said, 'By teaching pupils how to do or be competent at science (history, morality, and so on) you are "imposing values" on them', what should we say? In one sense, and one only, we are 'imposing values', or at least recommending them: namely, the merits of reason, intelligent thought, and respect for relevant facts. These values, if we must call them so, are built into the notion of education just as they are built into the notion of being human and conscious. But we are not imposing particular values – partisan moral or religious beliefs, specific attitudes to works of art, and so on. We are, rather, helping pupils to make up their own minds in the light of reason. So apart from being clear about what it is to educate someone, we need not worry.

One of two things must be true. Either:

(1) we have some idea of how to get right answers to moral questions i.e. some notion of what counts as a good reason and what does

not, perhaps something approaching a methodology; or
(2) we do not (maybe we think 'it's all relative', or maybe we are just muddled about what good reasons are in morality).

If (2) is found to be true, we have no right to be in the ME business at all. Thus, if a pupil says 'I'm going to beat her up because it's Tuesday/because I hate her/because she's black', or whatever reason you like, all we can say is 'Ah, well, that's a point of view'. Certainly discussion would be useless; serious discussion presupposes the possibility of progress via relevant reasoning, of getting nearer to right answers or truth; otherwise we are just swapping feelings. Nor would we feel we had the right to know what sort of examples to set (inspiration to give, etc.), since (on this view) we have no clue as to what can fairly count as a *good* example.

I do not think anyone seriously believes (2) (not even sociologists, if properly pressed). We have some idea how to do the subject, some grasp of what can fairly or intelligibly count as a reason, and of what we are committed to by the use of words like 'ought', 'right', etc. I think that we have a pretty good idea; that, at least on reflection, most sane people would accept that reasons – to count as good reasons – would have to be shown to relate to human needs and interests (rather than what some 'authority' says, or what one's inner feelings suggest to one, or what one selfishly wants, or what day of the week it is). If so, quite a lot follows: we need whatever skills, knowledge, abilities, aptitudes, etc. will best enable us to work out these reasons properly and act on them. My point is simply that if we do not have any rational agreement on moral methodology and reasoning, we are not in business at all: but insofar as we do, we ought to teach it to pupils.

A complete list of the bits of equipment (not 'skills') or components which a person requires if he is to be fully educated or competent in morality would include:

PHIL (HC)	Having the concept of a 'person'.
PHIL (CC)	Claiming to use this concept in an overriding, prescriptive, universalized (O, P and U) principle.
PHIL (RSF) (DO AND PO)	Having feelings which support this principle, either of a 'duty-oriented' (DO) or a 'person-oriented' (PO) kind.
EMP (HC)	Having the concepts of various emotions (moods, etc).

EMP (1) (Cs)	Being able, in practice, to identify emotions and moods in oneself, when these are at a conscious level.
EMP (1) (Ucs)	Ditto, when the emotions are at an unconscious level.
EMP (2) (Cs)	Ditto, in other people, when at a conscious level.
EMP (2) (Ucs)	Ditto, when at an unconscious level.
GIG (1) (KF)	Knowing other ('hard') facts relevant to moral decisions.
GIG (1) (KS)	Knowing sources of facts (where to find out), as above.
GIG (2) (VC)	'Knowing how': a 'skill' element in dealing with moral situations, as evinced in verbal communication with others.
GIG (2) (NVC)	Ditto, in non-verbal communication.
KRAT (1) (RA)	Being, in practice, 'relevantly alert' to (noticing) moral situations, and seeing them as such (describing them in terms of PHIL, etc. above).
KRAT (1) (TT)	Thinking thoroughly about such situations, and bringing to bear whatever PHIL, EMP, and GIG one has.
KRAT (1) (OPU)	As a result of the foregoing, making an overriding, prescriptive and universalized decision to act in people's interests.
KRAT (2)	Being sufficiently whole-hearted, free from unconscious counter-motivation etc., to carry out (when able) the above decision in practice.

(For a full explanation of these, see Wilson, J. 1973).

It might be said, not completely without justice, that all this presses the notion marked by 'education' far too strongly. Cannot the learning of a particular set of values or moral beliefs also count as ME, whether or not a desirable kind of ME? To this I offer three answers, two of a pragmatic and *ad hoc* nature, the other rather more philosophical:

1. First, we might accept this point and say – what is true – that we were interested chiefly, during our research in Phase II, in *our* concept of ME: that is to say, in whether the respondents could or did grasp the idea of a non-partisan ME (whatever other kinds of ME there were).

2. Secondly, in a world full of violence and conflict there are

obvious pragmatic reasons for preferring this non-partisan concept. Granted that each individual or social group has moral beliefs or ideologies of his (its) own, nevertheless the desirability of some kind of education which is, in a fairly obvious sense, neutral or non-partisan must be clear enough.

3. Thirdly, though here I plunge far too briefly into complicated philosophical topics, it might, I think, be argued that the implications of 'education' do in fact exclude or at least cast great doubt upon the learning of many substantive values. One way of questioning this would be to suggest that 'indoctrination' is a more appropriate term (if the substantive values are not based on pure and non-partisan reason, in which case we are back with our own concept). Another way would be to press the connections between learning on the one hand and truth, good reasons, and knowledge on the other. Education implies learning (not just *any* acquisition of values), and 'learn' usually implies that the pupil acquires some *knowledge*: and 'knowledge' implies not only that the values are valid but that the pupil has good reason to believe that they are. Any programme of ME which was ultimately based on some particular set of values (and not upon higher criteria of reason which might or might not justify these) could not meet these demands. The pupils might come to think that such-and-such things were good and bad, and come to act or avoid acting in certain ways; but that alone is certainly not enough for us to talk of education.

An Initial Inquiry

I myself, together with one or two members of the research team, had the advantage (if it may fairly be called so) of having been engaged in research into ME since 1965. During the course of this research, we had paid some attention to the problems of trying to determine other people's beliefs, opinions and concepts in the extremely slippery area of ME. These problems are not, I think, fully appreciated: indeed there are a number of books which purport to convey solid knowledge of how people think in this area but which used the (in our judgement) wholly inappropriate methods of formal questionnaires and other such instruments. The problems which we were to face in our later enquiry (see next section) emerged most clearly in an initial attempt to gain information by questionnaire methods. I shall summarize this here because they apply much more to ME than to discipline: the concepts and beliefs are far more confused and heterogeneous than they are in the case of discipline. 'Discipline' ('well-disciplined', etc.) can be translated, not indeed without difficulty, but usually without much ambiguity, into other languages. Although one can in a sense translate 'ME' unambiguously, there is a far wider variety of connotations and images connected with the term or its equivalent in other languages and cultures than there is in the case of discipline.

This initial inquiry was wide-ranging, and conducted internationally. Although ME must for operational purposes be defined (as we have tried to do) in a way which will stand up to philosophical criticism, it is plain that no comparative study of the aims or practice of various countries should restrict itself within the forms of such a definition. Thus, a refusal to consider (say) what happens to the young in present-day China, on the grounds that this looks more like indoctrination than education, would be a piece of philosophical purism, doing more disservice than service to the subject. Our general concern, then, is with that vague area for which 'ME' is only one title amongst others, such as 'human relations', 'l'éducation permanente', 'civics', and so forth. However, casting one's net as wide as this generates certain problems, as we shall see.

It was beyond our scope to investigate the comparative practices of ME in schools and elsewhere; this task would be a major piece of sociological research lasting for many years. But it seemed possible for us at least to approach a comparative study of aims: this, we thought, might in any case be a necessary preliminary to a study of the practice. To approach this study, in however amateur a way, we sent out a questionnaire to about 500 countries, which contained questions designed to elicit the respondent's concept of ME, the importance attached to it, its connections with religion, politics, etc., how far the respondent felt that further research was needed, and various other points that seemed to be interesting *prima facie*. We also spent a good deal of time in trying to analyse the various statements of policy made on this topic by educational authorities in the different countries, for which the literature is enormous.

These sources produced, of course, copious but very fragmentary and heterogeneous information. However, it was sufficient at least to begin on the methodological or conceptual problems that require (but rarely receive) attention before any serious sociological or comparative inquiry. These are chiefly problems about meaning and taxonomy, and I think they may be relevant not only to this particular comparative study, but to the many other comparative studies of educational aims in various subjects which are already under way.

A very naive inquirer might proceed like this: We want to know what the aims of ME are in Flatland. Very well, we send a questionnaire to the Minister for Flattish Education, and ask him, 'What aims do you have for ME?' He replies, 'To make good citizens and solid members of the Flatt Church'. We check this out by asking similar questions of Flatt headmasters, the President of the Society for the Moral Improvement of Younger Flatts, and so on – they say much the same. We then know what the aims of ME are in Flatland. Then we do the same for Cubeland, Lozengeland, and so on, so that we end up with lots of statements from various countries. We put these side by side, and there you have Comparative Aims in ME.

Now some of the naivety here is obvious enough. Do we know that the Minister for Flattish Education can speak for the aims of Flatland as a whole? (It might be plausible to say this about French Ministers of Education but not about English ones, for instance.) Does the agreement of the other Flatt respondents help, or are they all in league? And why should there be such a thing as the 'aims of Flatland' anyway? In the case of a small tightly-knit folk society or tribal society this phrase might be acceptable, but in pluralistic societies like the USA or the UK there might be all sorts of different aims corresponding to different social groups with different norms and ideas.

Less obvious are a number of problems which might be called logical rather than sociological. These require more careful attention.

(1) Are the answers sincere? Apart from sheer tautology, there are various kinds of insincere uses of language: more kinds than outright lying, as anyone familiar with the double-think of Marxist and other metaphysicians knows well. Many words and phrases, particularly in the area of ME, are used but not meant. They are lip-service, a tribute paid to the prevailing dogma or fashion. Thus the phrase 'democratic way of life' in western-oriented countries, and phrases like 'maintaining the revolution' and 'socialist culture' in some eastern countries, seem often to be largely ritualistic: no-one in Russia expects a good 'revolutionary' actually to man barricades. The post-war jargon of UNO and UNESCO documents seems to be either causative, or at least highly representative, of most of this ritual phraseology,

in the western world ('self-expression', 'right to development', 'the whole man', etc.), and is endlessly reproduced on educational brochures. Of course these may be sincerely meant: but they may be just parrotted.

(2) Are the answers meant in a normal sense? Even sincere answers may be obscure, and even after hacking through a 200-page jungle of verbiage about moral aims produced by the patently sincere, indeed ardent Squmpland Cultural Bureau, one may be pardoned for not really understanding what they are talking about. (It is sometimes as if the state authorities were anxious to combine the maximum of enthusiasm with the minimum of clear specification. What emerges is often not much less tautologous than A.E. Housman's, 'And O, my son, be on the one hand good: And do not on the other hand be bad'.) This comes out in two ways amongst others:

(a) terms may be narrowed from their normal sense: thus talk of 'immorality' or 'purity' may really be simply talk about sex;

(b) terms may be widened: thus talk of 'Communism', or 'the revolution', which may look very specific and partisan to a westerner, may in fact amount to little more than a synonym for 'desirable', or ' a good show'.

(3) Should one ask about ME at all? We said earlier that there were many different titles for this area of education. But this is very misleading, for there are different areas as well as different titles, and people are far from clear what the areas are or which titles should be stuck on to them. One respondent may react quite differently to the phrase 'ME' and the phrase 'human relations': and another may produce the same reactions but with the order of the phrases reversed. Many respondents said words to the effect of 'What do you mean, ME? All education is moral': obviously we should have asked them about the aims of education *sans phrase*. Others we should have asked about the aims of morality *sans phrase*. Without a fixed meaning for ME no simple questionnaire will be enough. Even the question 'What do you mean by "ME"?', apart from the paradoxes which arise when one has to translate the question in order to ask the Flatts, is not likely to do the job completely.

(4) 'The aims of . . .'; if they give an account of the 'aims', this account may be ambiguous between:

(a) an account of what their aims actually are, either in the sense that they think these aims actually to be incorporated in their practice, or at least in the sense that they try or intend so to incorporate them;

(b) an account of what they think, abstractly, ought to be done, without any implication that they are doing it, or trying to do it, or intending to try to do it.

(5) Whose morality? Respondents characteristically list a number of moral values, e.g. obedience, living a Christian life, and so forth. There is an ambiguity between whether the respondent means:

(a) that these are the values that they, the respondents, believe in and practice; or

(b) that these are the values which those being educated – the children – ought to believe in and practice.

Thus it is possible to hold that obedience is a virtue (an 'aim of ME') for children, but not particularly for adults. Conversely one might think that moral autonomy, or being a hero, was suitable for adults but not for children. (One might even think, as some people in our culture do, that children ought to believe in God, but adults should have grown out of it.)

(6) Means or ends? Respondents may list moral values in which they think the young should believe, but it is not clear whether they think the young ought to believe in them for their own sake, or for the sake of some (possibly non-moral) end. Thus a Chinese respondent lists 'obedience to the Party'. If highly metaphysical about 'the Party', he may think this is a moral aim in itself, but more likely, perhaps, he thinks that the young ought to obey the Party for some other end, e.g. to maintain discipline in the country and keep the economy on its feet. The difference here is that between *A* who believes in tidiness *per se*, as a moral virtue, and *B* who believes that one ought to be tidy (only) in order to be able to find things when necessary. This ambiguity runs through most statements of 'aims'. These difficulties are clearly not merely academic.

Whether or not one can hope to overcome them completely, one has at least to make up one's mind, in the interpretation of any particular respondent's words, on each of the issues and ambiguities mentioned above – and no doubt, on others besides that have so far escaped us. In principle one could only add to one's certainty over these issues by prolonged interviews with the respondents, backed up by the study of their behaviour and educational decisions. Otherwise, one can only hope to interpret each case by acquiring a kind of instinct, a nose for what the respondent is really talking about and really meaning. One may make more or less intelligent guesses as to the general mode of moral thought employed by those who talk of 'self-expression', 'creativity', 'developing powers of criticism', etc. as against those who talk of 'spiritual values', 'the soul', 'the highest good for Man' and so forth. But these are only guesses: to confirm them would require a good deal of anthropological research (a very worthwhile task, I should have thought, but not one that could in principle be conducted solely by observation of behaviour, statistics, or questionnaires). For we are here concerned with rational or at least semi-rational phenomena, and these require techniques of their own.

The remaining problems are problems of educational taxonomy: this is a subject about which, despite the conscientious if muddled efforts of various psychologists, there is still almost everything to be said. Here I confine myself to two possibilities. First, one might categorize these aims substantively, as I shall call it; that is, according to what seems to be the content or substance of the morality which they imply. Thus we lump together in one category all those respondents who talk of the virtues of being peaceful, humble, gentle, etc, and in another we put those who talk of fighting for the fatherland, dynamic leadership, and dying like a hero. Or, again, we conjoin those who hold values that might be called 'puritanical', and those whose values are 'liberal'. Secondly, one might categorize them logically, that is, according to what kinds of reasons are given, or supposed to be given, for the substantial behaviour advocated. Thus one might contrast conformist with autonomous respondents. The conformist category would then include those who advocate conformity to many varying norms or kinds of behaviour patterns (both sexual chastity and institutionalized prostitution). What makes it a single category is that the same type of reason is offered in each case, e.g., 'Children should be brought up to do X and Y because that is in accordance with the norms of this society'.

I take this to be the most important choice for the taxonomist in this and similar areas. Other categories (e.g. a 'frontier culture' morality, a 'folk-society' morality, a 'protestant ethic', etc.) seem to me premature attempts to interpret, and explain sociologically, categories independently shown to exist as such – premature, because I do not think they always have been independently shown to exist as such. It is one thing to show similarities in overt behaviour, social roles etc. and another thing to show similarities in anything one would normally call 'morality'; to show the second is to face the difficulties I have mentioned above. In other words, when once we have categorized different types of morality, and different aims for ME, in their own right, it will then be time for sociologists and others to show that it is no accident that moralities *ABC* fall into one category, and *DEF* into another (since different social causes are at work in each case).

Plainly a choice of taxonomy must depend on one's particular purposes. If one is interested in overt behaviour, one would adopt the former method (a substantive categorization), and if in the way people think and feel, the latter (a logical categorization). It has been shown often enough that for most purposes the former is dependent on the latter. Briefly, this is because it is impossible to characterize what people do (except in a very boring way, by spatio-temporal descriptions of physical movements) without reference to their intentions and reasons. This is not to say that for all purposes the latter is the better method, but it is likely to be more fruitful for the practice of ME, and therefore (arguably) for the comparative study of the aims of ME.

This does no more than pose the problems, and I would not wish to convey the impression that it is all clear what actual categories should be used. However, I would suggest two dimensions which seem to us to make some sort of sense out of the heterogeneous mass of material with which we are confronted:

(A) Conformity – Autonomy. This is (obviously) concerned with how far the respondent regards morality as connected with particular behaviour patterns on the one hand, or with freely chosen values on the other: hence, how far he is anxious to produce children who conform or think for themselves. Much, or course, may be said about the exact meaning to be given to 'autonomy', and about the (logically and substantively) different types of conformity.

(B) Social/utilitarian-ideological. This is basically a question of whether the respondent is concerned chiefly with interests, such as human welfare, injury, harm, benefit etc., or with ideals that may bear no relation to interests. Thus the idea of mediaeval chivalry, or the Japanese bushido, is not necessarily, though it may be (and certainly has been in the past), concerned with anybody's welfare or happiness, or (necessarily) with the good of society: it is, rather, an ideal of conduct and belief put forward in its own right. Such ideals may or may not be religious or metaphysical. What makes them ideals is that they are not defended by utilitarian considerations.

Further categorization should, I think, be concerned with sub-sections of these; for instance, with the kind of norms to which the young are supposed to learn to conform, the kind of ideal which is put before them (religious, humanist, political, etc.) and so forth. But it is plain enough that before we can proceed with this safely, we have to be clear, e.g., just what is to count as a religious (as opposed to, say, a moral or political) ideal. Into which of these categories do we put Marxism, Maoism, or Nazism? To answer this, we have not only to find out more facts about these ideals, but to be clearer about what we mean by our own categories. I am not saying that this is impossible; but it has to be done and done first.

After that there is, I hinted earlier, the task of ensuring that one's semi-intuitive interpretations are correct; that is, that what seem to be key words and phrases in the responses are in fact evidence of a particular mode of thought in the respondent. We are fairly optimistic about being able to show this in due course: and this is one reason, amongst others, why we shall be pursuing the area of study, and perhaps make a fuller attempt to evolve a set of categories along the lines already mentioned. The interest of such a study is no less than its difficulty.

Finally, and simply for purposes of illustration, it may be useful to quote (anonymously) some of the statements about which I have been talking. I print them here together with some of the questions which (in our view) any student ought to bear in mind when dealing with material of this kind.

(1) A selection of lip-service phrases, tautologies or near-tautologies (see (1) and (2) above): 'Well-rounded healthy personality', 'To challenge capitalism, colonialism, imperialism, feudalism . . .', 'versatile people who harmoniously combine spiritual health, moral purity, and physical perfection' (!), 'love of the socialist motherland', 'healthy discipline', 'wholesome habits'. Question: What do any of these mean? How sincere are these? What would they imply in practice (e.g. if you 'challenge colonialism', do you pick up a gun and invade Malaya, or just think in a different way, or what?)

'To educate children to live in a proper relationship with God, man and nature', 'The development of sound standards of individual conduct and behaviour', 'To provide moral and ethical principles on which to base the good life'. Question: do these mean anything?

(2) Conformist or autonomous?

'To make good citizens and good men', '. . . healthy personality and acceptable social behaviour', 'To make good citizens, to make children think for themselves'. Query: what happens if the two halves of these statements conflict?

'. . . the educational value of censorship . . .' (*sic*), 'to cultivate national values' (as the text from which this comes is full of misprints, it is possible one should here read 'rational'. This neatly illustrates one of the crucial distinctions which it is hard to extract from such texts).

(3) Means or ends (see (4))?

'. . . establishing standards and aims. To increase patriotism is of prime importance in the present situation' (*per se* or for ulterior motives? Here plainly the latter) 'Anything that takes us out of ourselves and inspires us to sacrifice for the good of others or for a great cause is of spiritual value', (Query: *anything?*), '. . . to teach the dignity of manual labour and patriotism', 'To combat wrong attitudes by making manual work compulsory in school curricula'.

(4) Utilitarian or ideological?

'. . . love of country and loyalty to the Throne', '. . . a deep faith in socialist ideals, loyalty to country and readiness to defend it'. 'This nation-building is aimed not solely at material development but especially at spiritual development. The ideology of nationalism must be the strongest among other ideologies'. Question: how far do these respondents want people actually to do things (i.e. fight, work) and how far just to admire an ideal? (Of course both, but in what proportions or with what priorities?)

These could be continued *ad infinitum*. I have taken extracts from those responses which are particularly ambiguous or difficult, and do not want to convey the impression that all or even most are so (though an amazing number are). Sometimes they come right out with an identifiable line, e.g. (1) 'the conquest of the child's own moral autonomy', or conversely (2) '. . . the school has . . . the authority of the state behind it to require of its pupils conduct in conformity with the accepted code of society served by the school . . . one of the functions of the school is to transmit and if necessary enforce acceptance of the mores . . .' or (3) 'to bring into the light the profound reasons which establish the unquestionable (*sic*) validity of religion, of Christianity and of protestantism'. (It is interesting that this extract, and its logical opposite (1) just quoted above, both come from the same country: thus rendering the question 'Does Flatland believe in autonomy or indoctrination?' unanswerable as it stands.) The comparative ease of identification makes the task a possible one. But the ambiguous extracts will, I hope, help to reinforce my main purpose, which is to draw attention to the logical difficulties in comparative educational study. ME is admittedly an extreme case: but those engaged on other comparative studies may find that the cap fits them as well.

The Findings

Partly as a result of this initial enquiry, we felt it likely that there would be as much (or more) confusion, uncertainty and variety of response in this area than in the area of discipline, so we decided again to adopt a two-stage strategy. First, we would try to tap respondents' *general* pictures of ME: in brief, to find out what ideas, methods, aims and other features were associated with the phrase 'ME' in their minds. Secondly, we would try a more structured approach, to see how far respondents understood and accepted what seemed to us the crucial features of a rational or valid concept marked by ME (as briefly defended earlier, p.91, with references).

   In the first of these tasks we were helped by some other research carried out earlier by myself and my assistants (not previously published) which was essentially designed with the same objective in view. That work was done solely with teachers: we now attempted, whilst keeping to the same interests and methods of approach, to expand it by including substantial numbers of parents, pupils and educationalists also, thereby making it parallel to the work on discipline described earlier. Interestingly enough, this expansion into other categories (non-teachers) did not significantly alter the kinds of responses we got: I mean, that teachers and non-teachers alike responded in much the same way. Indeed there was not much difference between any of the four categories. The implication seems to be that, since some categories are much clearer and firmer than others in their grasp of the concept marked by 'discipline', the concept marked by 'ME' is (perhaps unsurprisingly) much more obscure and confused: the phrase evoked responses or pictures which are, no doubt, much more basic and common to all categories of respondents. We could see the same pictures being produced by pupils of 13, teachers of 50, middle- and working-class parents, and educationalists of varying ages, qualifications and intelligence.

We proceeded, then, in the same way that we had done when dealing with discipline; that is (see p.27), taking the same four categories with about 300 in each, yielding about 1,200 respondents later reduced to 1,000. (None of these were the same respondents as those we had asked about discipline.) For Phase I, we used the data already existing on 300 teachers from work done at the Farmington Trust, and added the other categories, using precisely the same kind of unstructured interview. For Phase II, we used a new population of teachers (of roughly the same sort as the original 300) but the same population for the other three categories.

Phase I

The first and most important thing to be said is that the respondents' concepts of ME are *not clear*. This emerges in various ways. First, the concepts are often self-contradictory. For instance, when asked 'Do all parents have a moral right to bring up their children in accordance with their own moral or religious ideals, whatever these may be'?, more than 50 per cent said 'Yes': when asked 'What about the ideals of the Nazis, or the Communists, or the Jehovah's Witnesses?', almost all retracted. Again, many said that it was important for adolescents to be able to discuss moral problems frankly and freely with the teacher, but destroyed the illusion by adding, 'so long as they don't say anything too bad', or, 'so long as they reach the conclusions that the teacher wants'. Or they struggled with the twin ideas that the violence and cruelty in some books (the Bible, *King Lear*, etc.) were somehow 'bad', yet that those books were somehow also 'good'. These are, of course, difficult questions, and total clarity and coherence were not expected. In this the respondents show a confusion common to most of us.

Secondly, many replies to questions put under the title of 'ME' contained matter which did not relate to anything that would normally be meant by this phrase. This in two ways: (a) some respondents made little or no distinction between *educating* pupils on the one hand, and on the other hand doing various things to them roughly describable as conditioning, 'socializing,' training, indoctrinating, inspiring, keeping out of trouble, or simply keeping quiet; (b) Some made no distinction between the kind of advantages or 'goods' connected with education (roughly, advantages to do with knowledge, understanding, awareness and rationality), and quite different 'goods', for instance keeping pupils well-fed, healthy, happy, clean and economically viable. (One respondent said, 'For me ME means keeping the nits out of their hair', adding, 'though I suppose that's Health Education really, isn't it?')

This lack of clarity was not because of any particular stupidity or prejudice on the part of the respondents. It was plainly because, in common with the rest of us, they used the phrase 'ME' as a peg on which to hang their particular interests, fears, desires and fantasies. The incoming data was not properly describable as the *beliefs they held* about ME, as if 'ME' was a phrase clearly understood by all (as 'teaching maths' might perhaps be): it was better to be described as the *feelings or pictures* sparked off in them by this phrase. The words in which these feelings and pictures were first expressed would often be changed after some discussion with the interviewer, so as to become more sophisticated, consistent and apparently reasonable. The pictures themselves, if sometimes slightly shaken, remained (so far as we could see) essentially unchanged.

Categorizing these pictures properly would be a task for (amongst others) a clinical psychologist, and would demand far more time and attention than we were able to afford. There were some extreme cases, not too hard to identify. For instance, the remark 'ME? A good boot in the backside is all they need', or the more obviously Freudian 'They need their little bare bottoms tanned', allowed us to predict other responses with some security. Equally, 'It's a device of the capitalists to keep the oppressed workers in order', or, 'When I get to be a headmaster I'll damn well get the kids to rebel against this society: it'll be best for them if they look out for themselves and to hell with laws and morals', allows one to recognize the Thrasymachus-Callicles-Marx lines. But such cases were rare. More often one was lost in a welter of words, in which 'relationships', 'maturity', 'consideration', 'concern', 'integration', sensitivity', 'spiritual values', 'the Good' and 'social order' figured largely.

We had to proceed with great caution and in as non-directive a way as possible (it is interesting that a high proportion – over 90 per cent – said they would like to discuss it further, and that about 37 per cent of these actually approached the interviewer in order to do so, even though living in many cases at some distance away). For the lack of clarity already mentioned concealed, of course, a very high degree of latent anxiety and other powerful emotions in many respondents. Indeed it was possible to categorize them according to how easy or difficult they found it to answer questions and discuss the matter rationally at all. Though there were only two occasions on which the normal civilities ceased to be observed, there were many on which the latent emotions were not hard to detect.

Many had sufficient insight to be aware that their own emotions roused by the topic were of central importance (about 26 per cent made remarks to this effect without any prompting): this is reflected in the responses concerned with teacher-education in this field (see p.119). All this, of course, is extremely vague and inevitably subjective, but the points are worth raising for future research, and also because we cannot otherwise make sense of the actual responses themselves.

What we were dealing with, then, is not a series of philosophical views about the meaning of 'ME', but a series of pictures. Because of this, no clear distinction was drawn between *aims* and *methods* of ME: between the questions 'What is it to be "morally educated"?', and, 'How do we get pupils to become "morally educated"?'. The forthcoming pictures can be seen as a set of *models* of ME, incorporating both 'what ME is' and 'how ME happens'.

We were best able to classify these models under six headings, here described in order:

(i) *Contagion.* Many respondents talked as if morality or 'goodness' was a kind of object or force, which spread by contagion or infection. This was contrasted with 'badness', which spread by processes described as 'pollution', 'corruption', 'infection', etc. 'Goodness' was seen as flowing from 'good' teachers, parents, hero-figures, religious leaders or gods, into the pupil. A sub-division of this model stressed the notion of imitation and admiration of the 'good' source of power. Certain things, often connected with matters of sex or hygiene, dress, 'bad language', and even hair-styles, were regarded as 'bad' on a taboo-object basis.

(ii) *External authority.* Here 'goodness' consisted of obedience to external commands. Sources of the commands varied among respondents. Some spoke in a fairly pedestrian way of the authority of parents, elders, teachers, the law, etc., others of some religious leader (usually connected with the Christian religion, but a surprising number mentioned other religious authorities): others again of 'natural law', 'the spirit of the universe', 'the power of righteousness', etc.

(iii) *Internal authority*. This appeared mostly under such terms as 'conscience', 'what you feel yourself to be right', and so on. Goodness consisted of obedience to a number of internal commands, on a fairly strict analogy with obedience to external authority.

These three models had little to do with reflection, thought, or rational consideration of moral problems or decisions, and corresponded fairly well to the 'conformity' and 'ideological' dimensions mentioned in our initial enquiry (p.99). In some cases no question of *reasons* for obedience, or for accepting 'good' sources of power, arose at all.

(iv) *Self-interest*. The picture here was that pupils should be taught to be 'good' because it pays. Most respondents with this picture considered morality in a fairly pedestrian light, and were concerned with such vices as stealing, assault, murder and so on. The idea was to show pupils, that virtue – keeping the rules and considering other people – was a more sensible and rewarding way of life.

(v) *Socialization*. This model, sometimes proffered in the sociological jargon but more often in general terms, took ME as primarily concerned with fitting the pupil into 'society'. Usually 'society' meant 'England' or 'the UK': sometimes the pupil's future sub-culture, and sometimes the world (a few made references to the Common Market and 'being European').

(iv) *Love-and-reason models*. A heterogeneous bunch: but respondents here were concerned both with the pupil's autonomy as a thinking/feeling creature, and with the criterion of other people's interests. Much talk of 'sensitivity', 'awareness', 'thinking it out', 'concern', etc., seemed to suggest an interst in *education*, that is, the development of the pupil's understanding and rationality in the moral area. Few though had a detailed grasp of what this involved.

These last three models were much more concerned than the first three with the notion of *having reasons*, rather than merely with reacting or obeying, and corresponded to the 'autonomy' and 'utilitarian' dimensions (p.99), at least to some extent. Nevertheless, with the exception of some respondents with model (vi), a large majority (certainly over 75 per cent) were plainly worried about what many described as 'the basis' of morality, or else unworried because they were fixed up with a 'basis' already (usually religious). The models really represented different 'bases' which appealed to the different respondents.

Each 'basis' acted, in a confused way, as a power or authority source for moral beliefs and behaviour, as a kind of inspiration or strength-giving force, as generating a certain class of reasons for action, and as a touchstone or reference point for judging the actions of other people. We made no attempt to distinguish these, for they were not, for the most part, distinguished in the respondents' minds. The 'basis' served all these ends at once. It was as if respondents felt that there was a need for some unquestioned and unquestionable starting-point, set of axioms, or authority – something 'given'. 'We must believe in something', several said.

It was thus clear that very few (perhaps not more than 8–10 per cent) had any immediately clear conception of morality as an area of human thought and action which could be taken as parallel, in many respects, with other areas of education (science, history, etc.). A few younger respondents, brought up in a more modern tradition of educational philosophy, took morality as a 'form of thought' and could regard it without qualms as at least partly a *subject* which could be taught and perhaps time-tabled. But most, and all those addicted to models (i) – (v), saw ME more as the operation of 'brute' or 'spiritual' forces than as any *learning* process.

In particular 'moral' was, more often than not, taken as contrasted with 'immoral', and ME was seen as 'making pupils moral' in this sense. There was little conception of the moral, as against non-moral, area of thought and action, and hence little conception of morality as a subject which could be studied methodologically. There was, however, a good deal of uncertainty about this, particularly amongst those respondents who were aware of living in a pluralistic society, and who were personally uncertain of their own values. The general impression was one of groping after some sort of 'authority' beyond the normal procedures of human reason, but most respondents were not clear what sort of 'authority' they wanted. This, combined with awareness of the empirical breakdown (rather than the logical inadequacy) of many existing 'authorities', gave the impression of considerable lack of confidence, except amongst extremist respondents.

Of the variables used in relation to discipline (p.30) we used here only a few, partly because we felt (rightly, as it turned out) that the data here would be much more uncertain and hard to interpret than the data for discipline. We used, in fact, the variables of age, sex, type of school, social class and autism (omitting the influence of educational theory, the holding of posts of responsibility, and the tough-minded/tender-minded distinction). Uncertainty about some of the data makes it unprofitable, and possibly dangerously misleading, to offer a full breakdown in terms of the variables we did use. I give below only those results of which we felt tolerably certain, without the benefit of many statistics.

(a) Although of course respondents did not confine their thinking to only one of our six models or pictures, percentages assigned to each model (if we have to do this at all) would look something like this:

(i)	Contagion	12%
(ii)	External authority	18%
(iii)	Internal authority	5%
(iv)	Self-interest	20%
(v)	Socialization	31%
(vi)	Love-and-reason	14%

(b) Models (i), (ii) and (iii) overlapped considerably, as did (iv) and (v). Reasonable certainty can be claimed as to the rough proportions adopting a non-rational and non-reflective model ((i), (ii) or (iii)) as against a more reflective, 'utilitarian' one ((iv) and (v)), though within these two basic groups it was hard to distinguish. Possibly stringent 'content analysis' would help here. With model (vi), there was some overlap with all of the other five models, but respondents in this category were usually easy to identify.

(c) No difference was found in respect of the sex or social class of the respondent, but *age* was highly relevant. Over 80 per cent of those addicted to the first three models were over 40: and addiction to these (particularly (ii)) was generally correlated with age. Almost all those with model (vi) were under 30.

(d) Surprisingly, there was no close correlation between model and type of school. It was possible to determine that those connected with schools where pupils were 'difficult' or 'badly socialized' sometimes stressed models (iv) and (v), but usually with overt reference to their own pupils, not to ME in general.

(e) It seemed clear that those with the last three models were superior to the other respondents in terms of intelligence, sophistication and general rationality (though not necessarily in terms of clarity and incisiveness: they tended in general to be more vague but also more open-minded). This was most obvious in the case of those following model (vi).

It must first be stressed that these data tell us nothing much about the respondents' actual *performances* or results in their jobs, in the field of ME (in the case of teachers, parents and educationalists). In casual conversation, many respondents described what they actually did: this often appeared to be in complete contrast with their professed concept of ME, but very likely worked extremely well. Nor, of course, can a comparatively short interchange do justice to the respondents' concepts; and so the above is necessarily a series of gross over-simplifications.

Nevertheless certain conclusions suggest themselves:

(a) It is possible, to judge from responses by age, that a more 'utilitarian', 'rational' and (perhaps) pedestrian concept of ME is coming into fashion. Plainly this has advantages as well as disadvantages. Respondents in models (iv) and (v), and sometimes (vi), rarely referred to 'ideals', outlooks on life, or to religious or other world pictures, much stressed by respondents in other categories. Models (iv) and (v) accounted for over 50 per cent of the total.

(b) The proportion for model (iii), concerned with internal authority or 'conscience', was surprisingly low (5 per cent), and substantially lower than for model (ii) (18 per cent). There was in general remarkably little reference to attempts to inculcate shame, guilt, 'a sense of right and wrong', etc., but much more to giving pupils an *external* 'basis' of some kind. If this is at all typical of an increasing disillusionment with such notions, it is of considerable importance, particularly in view of the stress laid by some current research on them.

(c) Striking was the absence of 'hard' authority within model (ii); that is, few respondents spoke of obedience to particular (living) people or written codes. Many more spoke of 'the common wisdom of men', 'the laws of the universe', etc. The desire for, and belief in, authority was there but it was – so to speak – extremely *blurred*.

Methods of ME

Little or no attempt was made in the interchanges to explain what *we meant* by 'ME'; hence the remarks under this heading may be thought to indicate the respondents' concepts of ME as much as the prevalence or perceived value of particular methods. This turned out, on other evidence, to be true.

Three methods or features of school practice stood out as both prevalent and as valuable in the respondents' eyes. These are: RE lessons, school assembly, and informal contacts between pupils and teachers. Their prevalence is not surprising, since the first two are legally required and the third inevitable. But that these 'methods' should be perceived as of most value for ME is interesting.

Also considered to be very valuable (though not very prevalent) was voluntary community service. After these four, the next most valued methods included discussion *in time-tabled subjects* (English, history, etc.), some kind of 'house' or 'tutor' groups, and extra-curricular clubs and other such activities. Significantly less valued was a constellation of features including team games, prefects, form captains, uniforms, punishment and school rules. Very little-valued methods included discussion on general topics, impromptu acting and role-playing, and an elected ('democratic') School Council.

These results tentatively suggested what might be called a neo-conservative attitude to ME. The old-style 'public school' constellation of team games, prefects etc. seems out of fashion, but the striking thing about the most valued methods is that, for the most part, they are already 'orthodox'. That is, they are mostly accepted as part of the school structure – the structure is *there*, and is believed to work. RE lessons, school assembly, 'informal contact', time-tabled subjects – all these are already in existence. By contrast, methods which may seem newer or less orthodox, for instance, role-playing, a School Council, are not so valued.

Whether or not it is correct (and, if correct, whether it explains very much) to say that attitudes in this area are generally 'conservative', the interviews and informal interchanges showed clearly that the value placed on certain methods correlated with the underlying models or 'pictures' mentioned in the previous section. Asked why they thought RE lessons, school assembly, and informal contact were so important, most respondents replied in terms of the 'contagion' model, the 'external authority' model, or the 'socialization' model. In their view, these methods somehow infected the school with 'morality', or gave pupils some authority to look up to, or in some way persuaded or encouraged them to 'fit in' with the school community.

These three models, it will be remembered, accounted for some 61 per cent of all those interviewed. By contrast, those who saw ME more as a matter of the learning of particular abilities, decision-procedures, etc. tended to favour other methods. For example, many in this group considered one central ability for the morally educated person to be the ability to know what other people were feeling: these favoured role-playing and acting as one obvious *prima facie* candidate for developing this ability. They also favoured more clearly educational methods – that is, methods more clearly concerned with teaching and learning – such as general discussion, analysis of moral situations and practical moral problems, and so forth.

Those whose concept of ME was of a certain kind might, on prompting from the interviewer, be willing to entertain a different concept: this would almost inevitably lead them to propose or accept different methods along with the concept. In the interviews, four methods in particular were canvassed: (1) a non-academic house or tutor system; (2) discussion and language-skills; (3) direct education of the emotions; (4); direct teaching of moral decision-making in time-tabled periods. Few respondents did not think each of these important, but many seemed to prefer to view them under some other heading than ME, perhaps as part of 'emotional development', 'maturity', 'growing up', etc.

In general I would hazard here no more than the above (tentative) conclusions, which point once more to the dependence of methods of ME on the original concept or picture of ME.

An enormous variety of other methods was mentioned even by these few respondents. They include Outward Bound-type activities, discussions on particular moral topics (especially sex and the family), various kinds of drama, role-playing, dance, etc., a course on world religions, 'making the older girls wash up for old folk', different sorts of face-to-face relationships and counselling, taking the children on expeditions, and so forth. Outstanding by its unpopularity was any reference to school councils and 'school democracy'; but in general these methods were chiefly extensions of the 'orthodox' methods. Few of them were freakish or surprising.

It seemed clear that novel methods of ME were practised most intensely, and perhaps most successfully, in schools perforce concerned with their pupils' emotional and moral needs, and not solely or chiefly with their academic success. They are not, of course, confined to schools for maladjusted or delinquent children. However, the impression was that orthodox schools with reasonably well-socialized children could gloss over the task of ME, whereas schools in under-privileged areas, or with special problems – or of course with teachers who had strong concepts of ME – were far more likely to take it seriously and hence more likely to develop novel methods.

Fourthly, there was a strong emphasis on the pupils learning by 'doing' or by 'experience' rather than simply from books. Those interviewed on this point said that they would welcome *simple* literature that helped to anchor the various 'experiences' which they attempted to give their pupils, but expressed doubt about the merits of more 'advanced' literature.

Finally, there was a good deal of uncertainty about whether these 'little-known' methods actually worked, and a strong desire for them to be evaluated by researchers.

We did not come across (probably we should not have expected to) any methods of which we had not heard and read, but the results were nevertheless useful. One important point that emerged was the need for a wider dissemination of knowledge (or hypotheses) concerning these methods. Some respondents had, so to speak, been practising their particular methods for years until it had become an unquestioned metaphysic or way of life for the school, and it was important to prevent any new methods from becoming ingrown. Further, there was substantial support for the view that those who took ME seriously did not conform to the pattern of responses about 'orthodox' methods: they looked further afield, and realized that RE, school assembly and informal contact were insufficient. At the same time they, too, displayed a considerable lack of clarity about aims.

Practical difficulties

Sometimes, in the informal interviews, respondents (particularly teachers) were asked to mention these. Though those mentioned depended partly on the methods of ME they would like to adopt, or to use more fully, certain general points emerged.

First, and nearly always mentioned first, were difficulties which could not be surmounted by any short-term action: chiefly those arising from the home background and environmental conditions of the pupils, such as poverty, systematic delinquency, low ability in deferring gratification, and so on. Sometimes 'the state of society' as a whole was mentioned, with particular reference to the exaggerated importance of money, 'success', social class, etc. or to the lack of any 'faith to live by' in our society.

Secondly, however, *teachers* at least mentioned specific and, in principle, removable handicaps. These were, in order of importance (though we must remember the limited size of the sample):

(1) Lack of discipline;

(2) The pressure of examinations and academic work, which prevented enough time being given to ME;

(3) The excessive mobility of staff, which prevented long-term responsibility being taken for particular groups of children;

(4) Lack of flexibility on the part of local authorities, chiefly in terms of time, money and transport. (For instance, many headteachers would prefer to be more able than they are now to time-table their schools as they wish, spend available money as they think fit, arrange school buses to suit school arrangements, and so on);

(5) Legal requirements which made teachers more cautious about their pupils than they would otherwise be;

(6) Lack of proper buildings and equipment.

These observations seem to us striking. It was clear from these interviews that teachers would welcome much more responsibility and control of their charges. Many would like to cut down on 'academic' time, and devote more time to ME: some wanted to allot more money ('special responsibility' allowances) to the 'pastoral' as against the 'academic' staff. Almost all considered that inflexibility and bureaucracy on the part of the local authorities made it difficult to plan anything new or exciting in the field of ME, by way of re-time-tabling the school or by other methods.

No doubt some of these difficulties (e.g. time allotted to academic and particularly examination work) are partly of teachers' own making. Others too may be in reality the natural conservatism of teachers themselves rather than external impositions which they would immediately throw off if they could. Nevertheless it is clear (and in our view encouraging) that teachers welcome more control and independence, and a good deal more might be done in ME if they were given it.

Teacher-training

Responses here were heterogeneous, but in general results emerged which confirm the remarks on teacher-training in sections that follow. A large majority felt that it was the personality of the teacher that counted, and welcomed any teacher-training technique that would be relevant to this. They felt also that they needed more clarity about what ME was, and what methods did in fact fit it best; they believed that very many teachers would welcome in-service courses on these matters.

Many of those interviewed would like to see dramatic changes in the usual teacher-training programmes in Colleges and Departments of Education, at least so far as ME is concerned: believing that at present most that is done is of little value, consisting of vague discussion and poor quality 'intellectualizing'. Several said that there should be a clear distinction between (a) the academic aims and understanding of the subject, and, more important, (b) close face-to-face relationships with students and staff, in an endeavour to promote insight amongst the students. To this they would add (c) practice in dealing with many different types of pupils in many different 'emotional states', as one respondent put it, rather than just practice in subject-teaching.

In general, most respondents (again, in our view rightly) were disenchanted with most educational research, on the justifiable grounds that it did not tell them very much about pupils *as people*. When asked what sort of research they would welcome, nearly all wanted to know what methods of ME actually had what effects on what pupils (that is, they wished for research on assessment and evaluation). A lesser number were concerned with more abstract research on 'the basis of ethics', and very few wanted research on the more detailed techniques of teaching. It appeared plain that their chief desire was to have a serious and for-all-time assessment of various methods. Many stressed that they were fed up with the 'order, counter-order, disorder' that came from 'on high' in the educational world; that is, with the educational fashions that made constantly varying demands on individual teachers. They wanted research, but they wanted it to be of permanent value.

Many respondents asked questions about the tests and assessment methods that could in principle be used in this field. In reply to more direct questions, most of them expressed themselves dissatisfied with the usual criteria of delinquency, overt behaviour, etc. and wanted assessments which would tell (as one put it) 'whether the pupils were really better in themselves'.

Phase II

We applied here the same techniques as with discipline: to engage in longer and more directed conversations or interviews, in order to find out how easily various respondents could grasp or recreate for themselves the central concepts, and how they felt about those practical methods which seemed good candidates for (often, in my judgement, logically required by) the proper concept of ME. We were surprised by the extent to which this was possible, and to which even those respondents who had, in Phase I, seemed wedded to violently anti-rational or partisan concepts of ME were, under minimal guidance, able to entertain a more reasonable view. The difference between the Phase I and Phase II responses must surely be accounted for along the lines suggested earlier (p.103) – roughly, that certain compulsions and fantasies tend to inhibit rational thought on this matter, unless the stage is properly set for such thought. In other words, it is not that people *lack* the appropriate concepts or find them intellectually hard to master but rather that they are under internal psychological pressure not to *use* them.

The questions given (with 'response' figures) below are divided into two rough groups of 10 each. Of these, the first group is concerned with conceptual understanding, and the second with beliefs about the merits or demerits of certain methods. Since some methods at least seem logically required by an expanded concept of ME itself, the distinction cannot perhaps be sustained rigorously, but it would take a good deal of time to argue for the logical necessity of such methods, and we erred on the side of generosity in listing them as disputable.

Group I
1. 'Morality' as the title for a form of thought or department of human life; 'moral' as opposed to 'non-moral' (not as opposed to 'immoral').
2. 'ME' as 'education *in* morality' (not 'about morality'): i.e. learning what it is to be reasonable and to perform well, and actually performing well, in this department.
3. The foundations of morality not culture-bound or 'relative', or dependent on some ultimately unreasoned faith or ideology, but subject to reason.
4. There are good reasons for caring for other people and treating them as equals.

5. 'Ideals' (over and above their relevance to other people's interests) also a significant area of moral thought and action, and educable.
6. Education of the emotions relevant and possible.
7. Concept of a person, and reasons why others count as equals, important in ME.
8. Understanding of facts and feelings relevant.
9. Alertness and effective decision-making relevant.
10. Determination and effective translation into action relevant.

Group II

11. Teacher's own seriousness about morality more important than his particular moral beliefs.
12. 'Potent' schools (attracting pupils' emotional investment) necessary.
13. Classroom periods in moral methodology necessary.
14. In study and discussion, concentration on *clear* (not controversial) cases important, and cases within the pupils' powers to act on (not large-scale public issues about which the pupil may be able to do little).
15. A wide range of methods needed in schools.
16. Value of pupils' taking responsibility in real decision-making (e.g. administering school rules).
17. Classroom periods on 'ideals' (including religion) necessary.
18. Schools (not only parents) should take responsibility for this.
19. ME should be conducted internationally on the proper basis.
20. Importance of love and firm discipline as a foundation.

Specified responses
(percentages)

I		Pupils	Parents	Teachers	Educationalists
1.	'Moral' as against 'non–moral'.	87	63	74	80
2.	Education *in* morality	88	75	73	65
3.	Not 'relative' or ideological	64	86	62	37
4.	Good reasons for caring for others	79	87	76	74
5.	'Ideals' also relevant	46	53	36	32
6.	Education of the emotions relevant	47	38	46	64
7.	Concept of a person relevant relevant	75	69	73	54
8.	Understanding facts and feelings	92	74	94	86
9.	Alertness and decision–making	90	87	86	79
10.	Determination and action	74	90	87	74

II					
11.	Teachers' own seriousness	31	26	18	12
12.	'Potent' schools	68	48	37	20
13.	Classroom periods on morality	69	78	67	31
14.	Clear cases and within pupils' powers	58	77	69	27
15.	Wide range of methods	76	66	85	79
16.	Pupils taking responsibility	96	58	41	61
17.	Classroom periods on ideals	40	51	38	30
18.	Schools' responsibility	68	97	58	61
19.	ME on an international basis	97	68	74	89
20.	Love and discipline	99	89	68	77

CHAPTER SIX
Notes and Conclusions

What they wanted

In this section I am concerned only to state as clearly as possible
what most respondents said that they needed from units concerned
with research and/or development in ME, not with my own or
anyone else's views about whether these demands are right. Some of
this will have been evident in the data mentioned already: I will
summarize this here with the rest.

1. First, despite a good deal of confusion and misunderstanding, it
   was plain that the vast majority agreed with – or at the very least
   did not disagree with – the idea of a set of general, non-partisan
   aims. The notions of concern for others, insight, factual
   knowledge, self-control and so on were widely accepted, though
   often stated in different linguistic styles. Few on reflection wished
   to indoctrinate children with specific values or creeds which were
   the private property of particular churches, cultures or societies.
   Their hostility to this derived either (a) from the view that this
   was not the educator's business, and/or (b) from the view that
   such an approach would, in practice, be counter-productive, i.e.
   that to try to indoctrinate or force a particular set of values onto
   today's young people would merely make them hostile or bored.
   ('It's no good trying to browbeat them nowadays, you have to
   argue', or, 'Stuffing morality down their throats is the surest way
   to make them immoral', 'Look, if you want to stop them
   becoming Marxists the best thing is to discuss Marx with them: if
   you try to ban it or just say it's bad, that just makes them keener
   on it'.)

2. Their demands flowed from the above, and included:
   (i) *Clarification of aims:* many realized that words like 'concern',
       'sensitivity', etc. were vague and wanted a clearer understand-
       ing of these concepts, so that they could be clearer about the

aims in detail.

(ii) *Evaluation of methods:* above all, they wanted as much certainty as possible that particular methods did actually achieve the aims. Most of those interviewed were (perhaps surprisingly) very aware of how easy it is to *assume* that a particular method will work, *but be wrong*. ('We don't really know what works at all', 'Perhaps organized games and school assemblies don't do any good', 'Probably it's not *what* they're taught but *how* they're taught', 'We need some proper experiments here, not just prejudices and guesses'.)

(iii) *Practical material and methods:* they welcomed anything that could actually be used with pupils, provided it was properly backed by research and experiment: this not only (or even chiefly) for curricular material, but for methods concerning the social arrangements in the school, discussion sessions, out-of-school activities, and so on. Many teachers however expressed the view that they did not want (as one put it) 'any old person's view on what will help the kids: we're stuffed up with pamphlets and materials already telling us what to do, all very high-minded and no good at all. We want something that *works*'.

(iv) *Their on emotions:* aware that their own emotions, fantasies and prejudices vitiated much that went on in ME, a majority were concerned (though sometimes with some alarm or hesitation) to gain some form of training in this area. ('Our own emotions keep getting in the way', 'I don't feel secure enough to do some of the things I'd like to do', 'I expect a lot of what I've said is just prejudice: couldn't you run courses to help us see what we're frightened of?')

(v) *Bridging the gulf between academic and practical:* though few respondents (particularly those over 40) were clear about just what academic work had been done in ME, many were aware that there was some important work of this kind which they ought to know about. They wanted this 'brought down to their level'. ('We want to follow the experts, but we haven't time to go through the professional journals', 'Of course we must find out what Kohlberg has shown, but it's hard to get hold of', 'We're just amateurs – if only we had more time to study', 'Can't you write something simple to bridge the gulf between proper philosophers and psychologists and so on, and hard-working teachers like me?')

(vi) *More scope:* the demand is for more freedom for teachers to control their own school setting, time-tabling, etc. for the purposes of ME. ('I wish they'd give us a chance to get on with it.')

In some respects, or some areas, respondents were more positive (sometimes violently so) about what they thought was useless, a waste of time, or positively harmful:

(i) *Vague conferences:* most teachers – particularly those who were keen on ME, who had gone to the trouble of attending various meetings and conferences – expressed themselves highly dissatisfied with the vagueness of these events. ('I'm fed up with bishops and people telling us about the moral state of society', 'It's all too vague: can't we have some clear suggestions and actual experiments?', 'All the talk is far too high-minded, all about "spiritual values" and so on. If they had to deal with the tough East Enders I teach they'd soon see how useless it was', 'Can't we have somebody who really *knows?*')

(ii) *Bad research:* (see p.14) nearly all were 'fed up with the constant changes of fashion in education – so-called researchers telling us to do this and that without any real proof at all'.

(iii) *War between 'authoritarian' and 'permissive':* interestingly this emerged as perhaps the strongest feeling in those interviewed, particularly among teachers. Of this category only about 7 per cent took strong 'authoritarian' or 'permissive' lines, and regarded ME as some sort of battle against an 'enemy'. But even these (or about 5 per cent at least of them), when they spoke as teachers rather than as public commentators, joined with the other 93 per cent in expressing intense boredom and dislike of what one called 'the left-right war'. ('I can tell you that teachers are absolutely fed up with authoritarians and anarchists shouting at them', 'We want to get on with *teaching*: God knows I'm keen on morals, but there are too many people thinking they're God these days – who are they to say to us or the kids what's right and wrong?', 'We want some help actually in the schools, not a lot of telly programmes and letters in the newspaper'.) On this point one teacher, representing the majority opinion but perhaps more widely read than some, mentioned a passage from R.D. Laing's *The Politics of the Family*. The passage in full is:

As long as we cannot up-level our 'thinking' beyond Us and

Them, the goodies and the baddies, it will go on and on. The only possible end will be when all the goodies have killed all the badies, and all the baddies all the goodies, which does not seem so difficult or unlikely since, to Us, we are the goodies and They are the baddies, while to Them, we are the baddies and they are the goodies. Millions of people have died this century and millions more are going to, including, we have every reason to expect, many of Us and our children, throttled by this knot we seem unable to untie. It seems a comparatively simple knot, but it is tied *very, very tight.*

In general, it was quite clear that the respondents were concerned about ME, and anxious for research and development along the lines quoted above. But it was equally clear that they were hostile to vagueness, excessive high-mindedness, mere fashion, or being told what to do by pseudo-authorities who were not expert in the field. This applied, interestingly enough, even to those who might be thought to have some sort of 'obedience' or commitment to an established sectarian authority, for instance, those belonging to the Roman Catholic Church. Their criticism of much work (if 'work' is the right word) done in this field was its imprecision and practical irrelevance — 'waffle' was a common description. Many books, pamphlets, and other material were criticized on these grounds.

General conclusions

I give now some general conclusions arising from the data and relevant to the problems that emerge in it. These are based partly on common sense, partly on the consensus of academic opinion in the field, but chiefly upon the views summarized in the previous section. Naturally all those may be mistaken, but it would, I feel, be an unusually arrogant, ill-informed or autistic person who refused to give them their due weight. In what follows, then, I am not doing much more than spell out some of the obvious consequences of this informed consensus.

1. First, to repeat briefly the points made above, since concepts of ME are not clear, and often fantasy- or prejudice-dominated, we need:

   (a) further education of teachers and student-teachers in regard to the concept of ME;

(b) further education of them in regard to their own emotions and insight;

(c) classroom material for teachers and pupils which is seen to rest upon a clear concept of ME and a clear rationale.

Plainly these are not possible unless researchers and teacher-trainers are themselves clear about the concept: this seems a necessary preliminary to any serious advancement of the subject.

2. There is plenty of general concern for the subject. What is required is not the rousing of more concern, but the channelling of it along appropriate lines. Those wishing to advance the subject will not want to add their voices to already overloaded moral/political debates, but rather to attempt to increase the understanding and insight of teachers and other educators by the non-partisan processes of research, analysis and calm explanation; in brief, to generate light rather than heat.

3. It is plain that there is not enough clarity as regards either the concept or the methods of ME. The latter is largely appropriate, since in fact the actual *knowledge* (rather than guesswork or prejudice) we have about the efficacy of methods is very small. Teachers rightly resent being told to engage in various methods as a result of the hunch, instinct, or intuition of researchers and others.

Consequently only two general approaches seem viable:

(a) To proceed with the fundamental research required to attain such knowledge;

(b) In the meanwhile, to concentrate on those methods and approaches which are *logically* required by the concept (e.g. the development of language, improvement of discussion-skills, understanding of emotions, etc.). There seems little point in following prejudices about the merits of certain methods before the research has been done.

4. In general – and this may well have great practical relevance for research-teams and organizations – the prevailing lack of clarity, together with the urgency and importance of the subject, is likely to tempt research and development organizations into premature action. Nothing is easier, even under the title of 'research', than to attempt to spread one's own prejudices into the public arena (many examples of 'ME', so-called, in various countries are obvious examples of this). To do this will be to confuse teachers still further, and to discredit the whole subject. What is needed is harder, more intense and more scholarly work in the area. Whilst

we may legitimately encourage teachers to experiment, there can be no passing of the buck here: it is plain that teachers know, for certain, no more than the rest of us. They look to researchers to provide *knowledge* and *truth*, not to shout out their own views nor to add high-minded but vague 'waffle' to an already confused situation.

5. Tactically, it seems necessary to devise a practical training course for teachers for both the long-term (for student-teachers at college) and the short-term (in-service training, and short courses at Departments and other institutions). It may be that we shall have to wait for another generation of teachers before we can ensure general understanding of ME in the profession. There are, fortunately, some signs that the younger teachers are better equipped philosophically, and less (overtly) subject to prejudice, than previous generations. Meanwhile, however, a lot can be done to assist the thinking of contemporary teachers.

6. We require for this training courses rather than conferences: the latter often produce little but confusion and verbalized fantasy. The subject is far enough advanced for those well read in ME to transmit a clear and coherent logical and empirical content, even at this early stage. Public debate by the uninformed is not helpful here, however politically useful it may be for other purposes.

7. The focal point at which these needs become particularly obvious is the teaching of morality in classroom periods. A large proportion of teachers may be in favour of this, and there are in any case overwhelming arguments for it. Other methods or approaches to ME may be adopted, often successfully, without clear concepts, but the direct teaching of morality *as a subject* or form of thought and action requires them. A course or text-book for teacher and pupils would do a great deal to engender such clarity in the minds of both. Here too, of course, we must not forget the pressure of personal emotions and pictures. It may be that some would resist the clarity because it is too emotionally threatening for them, much as (or more than) some in the past have resisted developments in the study of science, medicine and psychology because they find it alarming. But this is an inevitable obstacle, to be overcome only by prolonged patience, encouragement and personal communication. Meanwhile, these results suggest that the time is more than ripe for a clear lead in this direction. On the evidence, most people would welcome something which is (a) clear and workmanlike, (b) non-partisan

and non-authoritarian, and (c) a good 'anchor' for other methods (role-play, literature, Outward Bound-type experiences, and so forth), (d) a good guide to moral methodology rather than a series of moral dilemmas or controversial topics.

To sum up: I have stressed throughout the absence of clarity about ME, and the strong emotional fantasies and resistances which the topic generates. This was very evident in the collection of the data, and in the data themselves. It is not peculiar to teachers; indeed there are signs that some teachers at least are among those prepared to take the subject seriously, rather than merely to act out their own fantasies and prejudices.

To take it seriously is to attend to the hard-won ground that has been gained from fantasy by the application of truth-seeking disciplines. We are at a critical point in the history of ME, in that such disciplines are now sufficiently far advanced to form a respectable corpus of knowledge. The philosophy of ME in the hands of Professors Peters, Hare, Hirst (see reference section) and others (including perhaps the present writer) is now an established and reputable concern, already accepted in most respectable universities and colleges of education. Some relevant psychology and sociology has also emerged fairly clearly in the work of Kohlberg, Williams, Wright, Argyle and many writers in the psychoanalytic school (see references in Wilson, J., 1973).

The critical issue is whether those concerned with ME are intelligent and unprejudiced enough to recognize this fact (plain to anyone who has worked seriously in the field, but easy to miss for the non-academic layman), and, whether they are willing to bridge the gap between this corpus of knowledge and what teachers actually do in schools. Not only personal prejudice but the current state of particular societies may easily cause us to swerve from this task. Much that is said and written is no more than a muted war between 'left' and 'right', 'permissive' or 'authoritarian', 'rebels' and 'conformists'. Teachers and children are the victims of this war.

Whether truth and its attendant concepts of evidence, rational thought, hard work and impartiality will ultimately prevail seems very uncertain. It seems quite possible that the intellectual ground gained may be lost in the advance of irrational anarchy or in a 'backlash' of the 'authoritarian'. At a time when the issue is balanced in this way, it is particularly incumbent on those concerned with ME to make sure that they themselves are committed to the notions of truth and understanding rather than to their partisan prejudices. For without this, any research and development in ME will be either time-wasting or positively dangerous.

It is, however, an encouraging sign that ME (like 'RE') is now virtually an established subject at many universities and colleges of good standing. Given time and goodwill, the serious study of the subject will doubtless penetrate the general public – provided the passions of 'left' and 'right' are not so strong as to prevent the public from paying due attention to the experts, and provided that the experts restrain their own passions. It is particularly important that there should be good communication-lines between practising teachers and competent academics in the field, lines more influential than those between teachers and public sages, protest movements, crusades, drives, rallies, and other instances of contemporary emotion rather than serious thinking.

Finally, I give below some quotations (slightly edited from the viewpoint of grammar and coherence, but with nothing added) from tape-recordings. (Permission was given provided anonymity was preserved.) These quotations may help to illustrate respondents' views on some of the more important points mentioned in the main text.

1. *On different models and language-styles*
   . . . like this conference I was at last year – people use such different languages. The bishop kept talking about 'spiritual values' and 'God's law' and 'faith', and the humanists didn't like this, they talked about 'concern for others' and 'caring' . . . in a way they were meaning the same thing, but they didn't feel safe outside their particular lingo so they couldn't get together . . . I mean the religious people seemed to think you couldn't be moral at all without God's authority and of course lots of teachers didn't like them saying that . . .

   My belief, based on 30 years' teaching experience, is that you have to start anyway with an uncommitted language which is 'understanded of the people' [this is a quotation from the introduction to the Church of England Book of Common Prayer] – no good talking to modern young people in terms of a religion they don't accept, all that about the will of God and the laws of the universe and such. You have to talk ordinary English and teach about love and kindness and so on . . . unless you make

progress there they won't even look at religion in many cases . . .
and isn't this right anyway? 'If a man love not his neighbour
whom he hath seen, how can he love God whom he hath not
seen'? I'd advise you to keep it down to earth for quite a long
time, if you want to get anywhere . . .

2. *On the arrogance of moralists*
Blokes like me get very cross with all the moralists and modern
sages who seem to think they know the answer, as if they were
God or something . . . usually they don't even know anything
about children, let alone morals. 'Young people today . . .' they
say, or 'student unrest . . .' or 'no discipline' – what the hell do
they know about it? They haven't studied it properly and read the
right books, they just get upset because they're frightened and
shout about it on the telly or somewhere . . .

Look, if you're going to try to bully teachers into doing just what
you think is right, you might as well save your breath . . . no,
well, you're not trying to play God so far as I can see, even if some
of the stuff you write is hard to understand . . . you've got to
prove to teachers and everyone as far as you can that your
suggestions actually work . . . Look, we had a school governor
who was obsessed with the idea of making all the boys read –
every day; well, I could have told him, most of them didn't
understand it and the ones that did didn't agree with it, and the
only result was that they got put off – for good . . .

Yes, as soon as I started teaching in school I realized it was no
good just *telling* them what was right or what they ought to do,
you had to explain and reason with them . . . I remember the
local vicar coming in and telling them that it was the law of God
(or 'natural law' or something, I can't remember exactly, maybe it
was a 'spiritual truth') that they should be obedient and sexually
well-behaved and so on, and one boy said something like, 'Well,
if that's how it is, I'm –ing well not going to obey that sort of God,
and you can take your "natural law" and – it: why *should* I obey,
you haven't given me any reasons at all'? . . . the vicar was pretty
alarmed, I can tell you, he didn't know much about modern kids
. . .

. . . I'm still surprised, since I happen to have read quite a bit of the literature – Hare and Kohlberg and Peters and your stuff and so on, you know, I've been doing a diploma course on ME – lots of people still go around speaking as if they *knew* what ME was and how to do it – and when you talk to them they haven't even read the elementary books on it! It's like people thinking they know something about science when they haven't even cottoned on to Newton and Rutherford and Einstein and so on. I can't understand how people can be so arrogant . . .

3. *On the 'moral vacuum' and teachers 'being given a lead'*
Certainly, most of us teachers know all about the 'breakdown in authority' all right . . . the danger is, people are so frightened of just leaving a vacuum – you understand me, I mean just letting young people drift about – that they may try to put some new authority in its place. That's what happened in Germany, Hitler came . . . You have to understand, both pupils and teachers want to be given a lead but *not an authority*. We all have to make up our own minds, we want help in how to make them up.

Teachers look to you for help, you know, it's a big responsibility . . . you mustn't expect them to know the answer, it's as much as we can do to survive from day to day, it's a hard job being a teacher . . . Surely what you want to do is to get the real experts to study it – I mean the psychologists and sociologists or whatever you call them, the people who make it their business to find out the answers, isn't that what you're doing? Otherwise you'll just fill the gap with your own prejudices and feelings, and that isn't any help at all . . .

Moral vacuum? I know what you mean, but you don't know much about children if you think you can fill it just with bits of preaching and nice books. My pupils have a 'moral vacuum', but the reason is that they haven't received enough love at home and attention at school – nobody's ever really tried to understand them and care for them. You ought to be looking at things like school councils, the house system, school counsellors, project work and so on – anything that will make them feel wanted and loved . . . If you really come to this school and faced all those unloved, insecure, untaught children and seriously proposed to make them all read the Bible – well, God forgive you, that's all I can say . . .

I hope you won't mind my saying so, but I'm very worried if you haven't got a proper psychologist on the job . . . you see, unless you're living in a dream-world the fact is that you've got millions of illiterate, unthinking, rebellious pupils who see themselves as failures and as 'anti' the authorities . . . now if you really claim to be interested in helping them to be moral or even to be human beings, then that's what psychology studies, isn't it? You've got to find out the basic needs that aren't being satisfied, which means experiments and a lot of hard research – of course simple people like me won't understand all the work, but we desperately need the results . . . of course it's a long business.

4. *On communication and prejudice*
The truth is we're all scared stiff. We see things going on in society that we don't like, so we get scared and we run for cover; some run to the Church, some to Marxism, some to psychiatrists and so on . . . then we all get into our little groups and think that only *we* are right, all the rest are enemies, like in a war. There isn't much communication, people don't *trust* each other.

No, I think the only sort of conference that's any good is where there are definite questions and people properly qualified to answer them, otherwise it's just a lot of talk . . . What we want is the answer to questions like "How do children come to see that other people are important"?, "How do children learn to discuss and argue sensibly instead of fighting"?. "What effect does pop music actually have"? We don't know the answers yet, though an awful lot of people seem to think they do! . . . well, it's because they don't feel secure unless they think they do know, isn't that it? Admitting ignorance even to yourself is unnerving, isn't it? Surely these are very difficult psychological questions, they need a lot of hard work to answer . . .

Oh, we all suffer from prejudice, or worse – most people are fanatics about it really. The only ways you can keep sane is – there are two really – first, look at actual children and what they need, in real life, and second, keep yourself glued to logic and the facts, don't give your prejudices a chance to sneak in . . . it's very hard, not many people can even argue reasonably . . . most don't even try, I suppose nobody's ever educated them to do it . . .

The kind of communication you need is to make the findings of the experts intelligible to ordinary teachers . . . trouble is, a lot of people pose as experts who aren't really . . . I don't read anything myself that isn't written by somebody with a good degree from a proper university; luckily living near – University I can ask the people who really know . . . teachers are getting fed up with a lot of amateur rubbish . . .

A final note: these results were very encouraging to me personally in my capacity as Research Supervisor for the Warborough Trust. For, although there was obviously a great deal of work to be done by way of clarifying people's concept of ME (as well as other tasks), it seemed clear that the Trust's work was based on the right sort of principles. That is, briefly, we were correct in adopting a non-partisan (non-sectarian) approach, in trying to apply the very highest standards of academic (and particularly philosophical) scholarship to the research, and stressing the importance of the 'pieces of equipment' which could be shown to be logically required by any morally educated person. That approach seemed well in line with the bulk of public opinion, uncertain and unpractised though individuals often were in formulating their views. However, how far we or other similar bodies could suceed in getting our message across is partly a political matter, to do with funding, publicity and public relations generally. That topic is outside the scope of this book, but we have appended a brief postscript which may interest those readers who are concerned as we are, to translate our work into action.

Reactions to the Research Model

There is an important connection between what we have roughly called the 'relativist' state of mind about authority, discipline and ME on the one hand, and educational research on the other. Most, indeed almost all, educational research forswears any attempt even to clarify, let alone show the conceptual necessity of, certain educational objectives. Researchers characteristically take statements of goods or *desiderata* in education from elsewhere, from political authorities, parents, teachers, a 'general consensus', current fashion, or even (in one or two more grotesque cases) the pupils themselves. 'Who are we' (the story goes) 'to impose *our* values? In a democratic community . . .', and so on.

I have explained at greater length elsewhere (Wilson, J. 1972, 1979a) the various reasons why this is wholly disastrous. Here it seems appropriate to suggest that the chief reason, or at least one reason, why the policy is almost universally adopted may be simply that the researchers themselves – at least in the area of educational goods – are flirting with, if not actually wedded to, a relativist state of mind. The unconscious, or semi-conscious, or even sometimes wholly conscious, thought may be something like, 'It's not really possible, even in principle, to show certain objectives or values to be required or necessary in education: so the only thing we *can* do is to accept other people's, or just take as given whatever happens to be around'.

People in this state of mind, as we have seen earlier, will characteristically be unable to tolerate separation and therefore anxious to create some sort of solidity by 'integrating' or 'bringing together' – at the political level, rather than the level of rational enquiry – as many parties as possible. This results very quickly in what might be called 'committee research' or 'research by consensus'. The researcher becomes a research politician: he finds it necessary to collate many different parties in order to gain trust, confidence and what passes for intellectual respectability. Any kind of research on schools, for instance, will involve the consent and cooperation of parents, teachers, headteachers, teachers' unions, local authorities, county and city advisers, school governors, perhaps the inspectorate and the DES, and so forth. Many or all of these are likely to have interests not coextensive with, and sometimes directly inimical to, rational inquiry. Hence the research itself becomes politicized; and it becomes natural to derive objectives from a 'consensus', if not from the opinions or interests of the most powerful parties present.

In other words, if there is no established intellectual authority or expertise – if, perhaps, even the concept of such expertise is denied or has disappeared – then the business of research becomes a political free-for-all: just as the business of education and schooling becomes a free-for-all without a firm grasp of much the same concepts. There is, of course, no particular surprise here: the concept of authority has such wide application that its absence would have similar results in almost any enterprise or field of cooperative endeavour. But unless we recover it, serious educational research becomes virtually impossible: research will simply reflect current climates or power stuctures.

We had something like the above considerations in mind when deciding to show some of our findings and conclusions to various people before publication. About fifty subjects were selected (also of course to remain anonymous), and given the main outline and arguments of this book. The reactions we were trying to elicit were to the *general procedure* of our work, not to this or that particular point: and in fact we found it quite hard, in many cases, to elicit this, since a lot of people could only be construed as *not wanting to face* the question of whether this procedure was right or appropriate. By this I mean, not that they were too lazy or busy to spend time and effort on the question, nor that they were bored by it, nor even that they thought it in some simple sense 'unimportant': one might rather say that they found it too alarming, too unlike the world as they knew it. A typical conversation (schematized and simplifed here), was:

Q: What do you think of the way we went to work?
A: Well, it's very unusual, isn't it?
Q: Perhaps it is, but do you think it's right?

A: Well, it's not like most research, is it? I mean, you've just said what *you* think discipline and ME are and why they're necessary, but perhaps teachers and other people think differently.

Q: Yes, indeed; but do you think one has to try to get clear about what discipline and ME really are in the first place (whether or not we've got it right), or not? What would you do if you had to do some research on this?

A: You say 'what discipline and ME really are', but isn't that just your opinion? I mean, there isn't anything which they 'really are', is there?

Q: Do you mean one person's got as much right as another to mean whatever he wants to mean by words?

A: Well, yes, it's all subjective, isn't it? So all you can do really is to just take what teachers and other people say it is, and that's what it is.

Q: But if a teacher said discipline meant doing exactly what one wanted all the time, surely he'd be wrong?

A: Ah, but that's an extreme case.

Q: How would one start doing the research then?

A: Well, I suppose you have to start by making up your mind somehow what discipline and ME are, and take it from there.

Q: How does one go about making up one's mind?

A: Well, that's difficult, I suppose there's some sort of consensus . . .

The fear which overshadows this and many other conversations is clearly that it is somehow dangerous or alarming to propound any sort of 'right answer' about educational objectives. Researchers can be wrong, teachers can be wrong, everybody can be wrong: and although 'wrong' makes no sense unless there are in principle 'right answers', it seems safer not to try to get them by the usual processes of rational argument and analytic enquiry. It is less alarming to pretend to oneself and to others that there is no such thing as being right or wrong: that seems more 'democratic', less 'authoritarian', more politically acceptable, less alienating and separating ('divisive').

Those who had the nerve (if this is the right word) to see that any serious researcher has to take the apparently more alarming course were nevertheless often reluctant to approve the procedure: not on the grounds that it was irrational or intellectually mistaken, but on the grounds that it was politically unwise or ineffective. A particularly interesting (and typical) conversation, which I give here more or less verbatim, makes most of the points clear:

Q: Do you approve our procedure, then?

A: Well, I suppose as a piece of pure research it's all right, but it'll upset a lot of people. The educationalists or administrators or whatever you call them will fight back.

Q: I'm afraid we're not very interested in that.

A: That's just what I mean! There you are, sitting in Oxford – there's a real world outside, you know – saying you're not interested in people's reactions – well, what do you think you're doing? Are you trying to help things on or just cause a stir?

Q: We're not really interested in causing a stir either; it seems that research ought to be concerned with making things clear and finding out the truth.

A: That all sounds very high-minded, but what good does it do? You won't persuade people by just upsetting them.

Q: Then how ought we to have proceeded?

A: I think you could *think* all those things you've written, that would be OK, I mean I agree they're more or less right or true; but you shouldn't *present* them like that. If you want to sell your conclusions it's no good saying in effect 'We think these conclusions are right', nobody likes to be told what's right.

Q: So?

A: So dress them up in some other way. Say something like – and you could, since it seems to be the case – not 'We have proved by argument and analysis that . . .' but, 'Public opinion and the general consensus of teacher-attitudes have now moved towards the ideas that . . .' that'll give what you say some kind of authority or weight.

Q: You mean, we ought to give it the weight of general or public opinion, not the weight of reason?

A: There you are going on about reason and truth again. Nobody *listens* to 'reason' in that pure Oxfordish sort of way, it just makes them gnash their teeth, don't you understand? The whole idea of research, particularly 'Oxford' style, is anathema to lots of people. If I were you I'd rewrite it and delete the Oxford image and get it backed up by all the right people in the teachers' unions and Schools Council and so on, then it might cut some ice.

Q: But then the reasons for which people accepted it wouldn't be the right reasons, they'd just be deferring to public opinion or a consensus or the influence of those in high places or whatever.

A: Do you really mind *what* reasons people accept it for?

Q: Well, yes, we do, because the kind of goods or *desiderata* we're interested in are bound up with people understanding them and accepting them as goods for the right reasons. I suppose if one played politics one could add to the weight of some 'authoritarian backlash' or something of that kind, and this might perhaps produce more general toughness or control: but it wouldn't produce more people who could *educate* and be educated *in* discipline and authority and so on. The right sort of reasons are essential for our purpose.

A: Very well. But even to get these reasons *listened to*, wouldn't it help to have some effective political or public relations backing? Isn't it just a sort of irrational puritanism which makes you deny this – as if getting political support somehow meant getting your hands dirty or sailing under false colours or something?

Q: H'm, yes, I think you may have something there. But perhaps we can defend this particular exercise on the grounds that we just didn't have time or ability to go in for this large-scale PR and politics stuff.

A: Or inclination, I should guess.

Q: All right, or inclination either. But not everyone can or wants to be everything: there's a place for *some* independent, non-politically geared-up work, surely.

A: Oh, yes, of course I agree. Maybe quite a lot of people will need it, and some of those understand it, and some of those do something about it. And yes, that's certainly better than just helping to create or joining in another flurry of fashion in education. But later on you'll have to organize the PR and politics somehow. Personally, I admire your impetus and optimism: anyone who wants to sell reason has a hard time of it.

Q: It's not quite so bad as that: I mean, fashion and politics and unreason and the pop world generally are so boring, it's much more fun trying to get things right. But the real point is – and I think our findings show it – that quite a lot of people *are*, at some level, quite reasonable enough about all this: they just lack the nerve and the clarity, and it may help a bit to support them.

A: Well, the best of luck. But don't expect any quick results.

Q: Good heavens, no, only a lunatic would think that reason exercised much power in fact over education or indeed life generally. But that only makes it more important to help things on a bit.

A: But it *is* really a bit arrogant, isn't it, to say that *you* know what's reasonable?

Q: No. First, of course other people may know too, and secondly, of course we may be wrong and then we hope someone will come and argue and get things clearer – that would be marvellous as long as there's genuine argument, and not just reaction. If you can get chaps really *arguing*, trying to find the truth, rather than just reacting, the battle's more or less won, because the truth will appear without the need for particular people to spell it out 'arrogantly', as you put it.

A: But people don't like arguing, in your sense: to most people 'arguing' means 'quarrelling'.

Q: Alas, you may be right: but that takes us into much wider fields.

References and Selected Reading

The literature on discipline and ME is enormous, though most of it is not based on a clear grasp of the appropriate concepts. We list here a very few works which should be useful to those who have some appreciation of the methodological difficulties.

ARISTOTLE (translated by J.A.K. Thomson) (1953). *Nicomachean Ethics*. London: Penguin Books.

AUSTIN, J.L. (1961). *Philosophical Papers*. Oxford: Oxford University Press.

HARE, R.M. (1963). *Freedom and Reason*. Oxford: Oxford University Press.

HARRE, R. and SECORD, R.F. (1972). *The Explanation of Social Behaviour*. Oxford: Blackwell.

HIRST, P.H. (1974). *Moral Education in a Secular Society*. London: University of London Press.

MISCHEL, R. (ed) (1971). *Cognitive Development and Epistemology*. New York: Academic Press.

MISCHEL, R. (ed) (1974). *Understanding Other Persons*. Oxford: Blackwell.

PETERS, R.S. (1966). *Ethics and Education*. London: Allen & Unwin.

SIZER, N.F. and SIZER, T.R. (ed) (1970). *Moral Education*. Cambridge, Mass: Harvard University Press.

TAYLOR, M. (ed) (1975). *Progress and Problems in Moral Education*. Slough: NFER.

WILLIAMS, N. (1970). *The Moral Development of Children*. London: Macmillan.

WILSON, J. (1972). *Philosophy and Educational Research*. Slough: NFER

WILSON, J. (1973). *The Assessment of Morality*. Slough: NFER.

WILSON, J. (1979a). *Preface to the Philosophy of Education*.

London: Routledge.
WILSON, J. (1979b). *Fantasy and Common Sense in Education.*
Oxford: Martin Robertson.
WILSON, P.S. (1971). *Interest and Discipline in Education.* London:
Routledge.

Index